WeightWatchers®

Best-Ever
Desserts

150 CAKES, PIES, COOKIES, BARS, BREADS & TARTS

About Weight Watchers

Weight Watchers International, Inc. is the world's leading provider of weight management services, operating globally through a network of Company-owned and franchise operations. Weight Watchers holds over 48,000 weekly meetings, where members receive group support and education about healthful eating patterns, behavior modification, and physical activity. Weight-loss and weight-management results vary by individual. We recommend that you attend Weight Watchers meetings to benefit from the supportive environment you'll find there and follow the comprehensive Weight Watchers program, which includes food plans, an activity plan, and a thinking-skills plan. In addition, Weight Watchers offers a wide range of products, publications and programs for those interested in weight loss and weight control. For the Weight Watchers meeting nearest you, call **800-651-6000.** For information on bringing Weight Watchers to your workplace, call **800-8AT-WORK.** Also, visit us at our Web site, **WeightWatchers.com,** or look for *Weight Watchers Magazine* at your newsstand or in your meeting room.

10-MINUTE TIRAMISU, PAGE 186

WEIGHT WATCHERS PUBLISHING GROUP

EDITORIAL DIRECTOR	**NANCY GAGLIARDI**
CREATIVE DIRECTOR	**ED MELNITSKY**
PRODUCTION MANAGER	**ALAN BIEDERMAN**
OFFICE MANAGER AND PUBLISHING ASSISTANT	**JENNY LABOY-BRACE**
FOOD EDITOR	**EILEEN RUNYAN**
EDITOR	**DEBORAH MINTCHEFF**
NUTRITION CONSULTANT	**PATRICIA SANTELLI**
RECIPE DEVELOPERS	**ELIZABETH FASSBERG, LORI LONGBOTHAM, MAUREEN LUCHEJKO, SARAH REYNOLDS**
PHOTOGRAPHER	**DASHA WRIGHT**
FOOD STYLIST	**MICHAEL PEDERSON**
PROP STYLIST	**CATHY COOK**
BOOK & COVER DESIGN	**DANIELA HRITCU**

ON THE COVER: Fudgy Cocoa Brownies (*POINTS*® value: *3*), page 64

About Our Recipes

We make every effort to ensure that you will have success with our recipes. For best results and for nutritional accuracy, please keep the following guidelines in mind:

● Recipes in this book have been developed for Weight Watchers members who are following the **Flex Plan** on **TurnAround**.® We include *POINTS*® values, which are assigned based on calories, fat (grams), and fiber (grams), for each single serving.

● All recipes feature approximate nutritional information; our recipes are analyzed for Calories (Cal), Total Fat (Fat), Saturated Fat (Sat Fat), Trans Fat (Trans Fat), Cholesterol (Chol), Sodium (Sod), Carbohydrates (Carb), Dietary Fiber (Fib), Protein (Prot), and Calcium (Calc).

● Before serving, divide the desserts—including sauces or accompaniments—into portions of equal size according to the designated number of servings per recipe.

● Any substitutions made to the ingredients will alter the "per serving" nutritional information and may affect the *POINTS* value.

● We recommend that all fresh fruits be rinsed before using.

CHOCOLATE-GLAZED CHOCOLATE
BUNDT CAKE, PAGE 26

Contents

Baking Basics

You don't have to be an experienced cook to consistently turn out delicious desserts and baked goods. You simply need to follow three simple steps:

READ through the entire recipe at least once so you will be familiar with the ingredients and equipment you need, as well as how much time the recipe will take from start to finish.

BEFORE you begin, measure all of the ingredients called for in the recipe. Allow enough time for items such as butter, eggs, and cheese to soften or come to room temperature. Set out the equipment you'll need too.

CLEAN up as you go along. Put away items you no longer need, place used dishes in the sink, and wipe down the counter.

Ingredients

BAKING POWDER Baking powder is a blend of baking soda, cream of tartar, and cornstarch. It is double-acting, meaning that it reacts first when mixed with a liquid and again in the oven when exposed to heat.

BAKING SODA Baking soda is used when a recipe contains an acid ingredient, such as buttermilk, yogurt, or chocolate.

CHOCOLATE In many of our recipes, bittersweet or semisweet chocolate can be used interchangeably.

COCOA There are two kinds of cocoa—unsweetened and Dutch-process—they are not interchangeable. Regular unsweetened cocoa is used along with baking soda to neutralize its acidity. Dutch-process cocoa, which gives baked goods a very rich, dark color, is treated with an alkali, which reduces its acidity, so it does not need to be combined with baking soda.

EGGS We use large eggs when developing our recipes. Avoid substituting another size.

FLOUR Bleached or unbleached all-purpose flour can be used in our recipes. Some recipes call for cake flour, which is made from soft wheat and produces the most tender cake. Whole-wheat flour is milled from whole-wheat kernels. Whole-wheat pastry flour is made from very finely ground soft wheat. Pastry flour is similar to cake flour but has a slightly higher gluten content.

SUCRALOSE A granular no-calorie sweetener sold under the brand name Splenda.

SUGAR Most of our recipes call for white granulated sugar. Confectioners' sugar is very finely ground sugar that is mixed with cornstarch. Light brown sugar and dark brown sugar is granulated sugar with molasses added.

How to Measure Ingredients

If you measure carefully and correctly, you will get consistent results each time you cook.

BUTTER The wrapper that butter comes in is premarked for tablespoons, $1/4$ cup, $1/3$ cup, and $1/2$ cup, so there is no need to measure it.

DRY INGREDIENTS Use standard dry measuring cups that come in nesting sets of $1/4$, $1/3$, $1/2$, and 1 cup. To measure flour, first stir it to aerate, then lightly spoon into the desired size cup to overflowing. Level it off with the straight edge of a knife.

LIQUIDS Place a glass measuring cup with a spout on the counter, and add the desired amount of liquid. Bend down to check the amount at eye level.

BROWN SUGAR Use standard dry measuring cups. Firmly pack the sugar into the cup, then level it off with the straight edge of a knife.

SPICES, HERBS, CITRUS ZEST, AND EXTRACT Use standard measuring spoons that come in nesting sets of ¼, ½, and 1 teaspoon and 1 tablespoon. Fill the desired spoon with the ingredient, then level it off with the straight edge of a knife.

YOGURT AND SOUR CREAM Use standard dry measuring cups. Spoon the ingredient into a cup, and level it off with a rubber spatula.

Equipment Know-How

FOR cakes and quick breads, pans that have a dull finish, such as aluminum, produce the best cakes. Avoid dark metal pans because they absorb heat too quickly. If using a glass or ceramic loaf pan, reduce the oven temperature by 25°F so the outside of the baked good doesn't overbrown.

IF a recipe calls for a baking pan, use a metal pan, and if a recipe calls for a baking dish, use a glass or ceramic dish.

TO determine the size of a baking pan or dish, use a ruler to measure across the top from one inside edge to the other, then measure the depth by holding the ruler inside the pan and measuring from the bottom to the rim.

Baking Terms to Know

BEAT To combine ingredients using a wooden spoon, fork, handheld mixer, or stand mixer.

BLEND To combine two or more ingredients.

CARAMELIZE To heat sugar until it is melted and golden to deep brown.

CREAM To beat butter or cream cheese until creamy or butter and sugar until light and fluffy.

CUT IN When making pastry dough, to cut fat into the flour mixture until pea-sized using a pastry blender or two knives used scissor-fashion.

DRIZZLE To drip a glaze or icing over a cake or other baked good.

FOLD IN To gently combine a light mixture with a heavier one without losing volume.

MIX UNTIL MOISTENED To combine a liquid with dry ingredients just until the dry ingredients are evenly and thoroughly moistened. The mixture is often lumpy.

SOFTEN Recipes often call for softened butter for easy blending or beating. Leave butter out at room temperature for about 30 minutes or until pliable—not greasy or melting.

SOFT PEAKS To beat egg whites until rounded peaks form when the beaters are lifted.

STIFF PEAKS To beat egg whites until pointed peaks form when the beaters are lifted.

ZEST The flavorful, colorful outer peel of citrus fruit.

Cakes

Chapter 1

CARROT CAKE WITH
CREAM CHEESE FROSTING

Carrot Cake with Cream Cheese Frosting

HANDS-ON PREP 25 MIN   COOK 35 MIN   SERVES 16

CAKE

- 2 cups cake flour
- 2 teaspoons cinnamon
- 2 teaspoons baking powder
- 1 teaspoon baking soda
- ½ teaspoon salt
- 2 large eggs, at room temperature
- 2 egg whites, at room temperature
- ½ cup granulated sugar
- ½ cup apple butter
- ¼ cup canola oil

- 1 (8-ounce) can crushed pineapple, drained
- 2 carrots, coarsely shredded (about 1 1/2 cups)
- ½ cup dark raisins

FROSTING

- 1 (8-ounce) package fat-free cream cheese, at room temperature
- 1½ cups confectioners' sugar
- ¼ cup plain reduced-fat (2%) Greek-style yogurt
- ¾ teaspoon vanilla extract
- ¼ cup walnuts, chopped

1 Preheat the oven to 350°F. Spray two 8-inch round cake pans with nonstick spray. Line with wax-paper rounds; spray with nonstick spray.

2 Whisk together the cake flour, cinnamon, baking powder, baking soda, and salt in a medium bowl; set aside. With an electric mixer on high speed, beat the eggs and egg whites in a large bowl until thickened, about 2 minutes. Gradually add the granulated sugar, beating until light and fluffy, about 3 minutes. Reduce the speed to low. Beat in the apple butter and oil just until blended. Add the flour mixture and beat just until blended. Stir in the pineapple, carrots, and raisins.

3 Divide the batter evenly between the pans. Bake until a toothpick inserted into the center comes out clean, about 35 minutes. Let cool in the pans on racks 10 minutes. Invert the layers onto racks and remove the wax paper; let cool completely.

4 To make the frosting, with an electric mixer on high speed, beat the frosting ingredients in a medium bowl until smooth, about 1 minute.

5 Place 1 cake layer, rounded side down, on a serving plate. With a narrow metal spatula, spread ⅓ cup of the frosting over the layer. Top with the remaining layer, rounded side up. Spread the remaining frosting over the top and side of the cake. Sprinkle the walnuts on top of the cake.

PER SERVING (¹⁄₁₆ of cake): 186 Cal, 6 g Fat, 1 g Sat Fat, 0 g Trans Fat, 28 mg Chol, 299 mg Sod, 30 g Carb, 1 g Fib, 4 g Prot, 56 mg Calc. **POINTS** value: **4.**

Food Note Greek-style yogurt, which is available in some supermarkets and in specialty food stores, is a rich-tasting, thick yogurt with the lush consistency of sour cream.

Apricot Cake with Pecan Crunch Topping

HANDS-ON PREP 20 MIN   COOK 35 MIN   SERVES 20

TOPPING

¼ cup chopped pecans

3 tablespoons all-purpose flour

3 tablespoons packed light brown sugar

2 tablespoons canola oil

½ teaspoon cinnamon

CAKE

2 cups all-purpose flour

2 teaspoons baking powder

1 teaspoon cinnamon

½ teaspoon baking soda

3 large eggs

1 cup packed light brown sugar

1 cup apple butter

⅓ cup canola oil

1 teaspoon vanilla extract

½ cup dried apricots, finely chopped

½ cup chopped pitted dates

1 Preheat the oven to 350°F. Line an 8-inch square baking pan with foil, allowing the foil to extend over the rim of the pan by 2 inches. Spray with nonstick spray.

2 To make the topping, stir together the topping ingredients in a small bowl until moistened; set aside.

3 To make the cake, whisk together the flour, baking powder, cinnamon, and baking soda in a medium bowl; set aside. With an electric mixer on high speed, beat the eggs in a large bowl until thickened, about 2 minutes. Gradually add the brown sugar, beating until light and fluffy, about 3 minutes. Reduce the speed to low. Beat in the apple butter, oil, and vanilla until combined. Add the flour mixture and beat just until blended. Stir in the apricots and dates.

4 Pour the batter into the pan; sprinkle evenly with the topping. Bake until a toothpick inserted into the center comes out clean, 35–40 minutes. Let cool completely in the pan on a rack. Lift out using the foil as handles.

PER SERVING (1/20 of cake): 214 Cal, 7 g Fat, 1 g Sat Fat, 0 g Trans Fat, 32 mg Chol, 95 mg Sod, 36 g Carb, 2 g Fib, 2 g Prot, 53 mg Calc. **POINTS** value: **4.**

How We Did It   Lightly spraying a knife with nonstick spray before chopping dried fruits, such as apricots and dates, prevents the fruits from sticking to the knife as you chop them. If you prefer to "chop" dried fruits with kitchen scissors, the blades can also be sprayed with nonstick spray.

Banana Spice Cake with Coconut Frosting

HANDS-ON PREP 25 MIN   COOK 30 MIN   SERVES 16

CAKE

- 2 cups all-purpose flour
- ¾ cup granulated sugar
- 2 teaspoons cinnamon
- 2 teaspoons baking powder
- ½ teaspoon baking soda
- ½ teaspoon salt
- ¾ cup low-fat buttermilk
- 2 ripe medium bananas, mashed (1 cup)
- 2 large eggs
- 1 egg white
- ⅓ cup canola oil
- 1 teaspoon vanilla extract

FROSTING

- 1 (8-ounce) package light cream cheese (Neufchâtel), at room temperature
- ½ cup confectioners' sugar
- 3 tablespoons light (reduced-fat) coconut milk
- 1 teaspoon coconut extract
- ½ teaspoon vanilla extract
- ¼ cup sweetened flaked coconut, toasted

1   Preheat the oven to 350°F. Spray a 9 x 13-inch baking pan with nonstick spray.

2   To make the cake, whisk together the flour, granulated sugar, cinnamon, baking powder, baking soda, and salt in a medium bowl. Whisk together the remaining cake ingredients in a separate medium bowl. Gradually add the banana mixture to the flour mixture, stirring just until blended.

3   Pour the batter into the pan. Bake until a toothpick inserted into the center comes out clean, 30–35 minutes. Let cool in the pan on a rack 10 minutes. Run a thin knife around the cake to loosen it from the pan. Remove from the pan and let cool completely on the rack.

4   Meanwhile, to make the frosting, with an electric mixer on high speed, beat all the frosting ingredients except the coconut in a medium bowl until smooth, about 1 minute. With a narrow metal spatula, spread the frosting over the top of the cake; sprinkle with the coconut.

PER SERVING (¹⁄₁₆ of cake): 227 Cal, 10 g Fat, 4 g Sat Fat, 0 g Trans Fat, 38 mg Chol, 259 mg Sod, 31 g Carb, 1 g Fib, 5 g Prot, 68 mg Calc. **POINTS** value: **5.**

How We Did It   To toast coconut, put it in a nonstick skillet over low heat. Cook, stirring frequently, until fragrant and lightly browned, about 3 minutes. Immediately transfer the coconut to a bowl, as the coconut will continue to toast from the residual heat in the skillet.

Apple-Cranberry Upside-Down Cake

HANDS-ON PREP 25 MIN   COOK 45 MIN   SERVES 12

¼ cup packed light brown sugar
2 tablespoons unsalted light butter
1 teaspoon fresh lemon juice
2 Golden Delicious apples, peeled, halved, cored,
   and cut into ¼-inch-thick slices (about 2 cups)
2 tablespoons water
⅓ cup dried cranberries
1¼ cups all-purpose flour
¼ cup granulated sugar
1 teaspoon baking powder
½ teaspoon baking soda

¼ teaspoon salt
1 cup low-fat buttermilk
¼ cup canola oil
1 large egg
1 teaspoon vanilla extract
2 tablespoons apricot jam melted
   with 1 teaspoon water

1 Preheat the oven to 350°F. Spray a nonstick 9-inch round baking pan with nonstick spray.

2 Combine the brown sugar, butter, and lemon juice in a large nonstick skillet and set over medium-low heat. Cook, stirring frequently, until the butter melts and the sugar is dissolved, about 3 minutes. Add the apples and water; cook, stirring, until tender and golden, about 5 minutes. Stir in the cranberries; remove the skillet from the heat.

3 When cool enough to handle, arrange the apple slices in concentric circles in the baking pan. Top with the cranberries and scrape any sugar mixture remaining in the skillet on top; set aside.

4 Whisk together the flour, granulated sugar, baking powder, baking soda, and salt in a medium bowl. Whisk together the buttermilk, oil, egg, and vanilla in a separate medium bowl. Stir the buttermilk mixture into the flour mixture just until blended.

5 Pour the batter evenly over the apple mixture. Bake until a toothpick inserted into the center comes out clean, about 45 minutes. Let cool in the pan on a rack 10 minutes. Run a thin knife around the cake to loosen it from the pan. Invert onto a serving plate; lift off the pan. Brush the top of the cake with the melted jam. Serve warm or at room temperature.

PER SERVING (1/12 of cake): 184 Cal, 7 g Fat, 2 g Sat Fat, 0 g Trans Fat, 24 mg Chol, 172 mg Sod, 28 g Carb, 1 g Fib, 3 g Prot, 57 mg Calc. **POINTS** value: **4.**

Zap It   A microwave oven makes quick work of melting fruit jam to a silky consistency. Combine the jam and water (or use fresh lemon juice) in a custard cup. Microwave on High until bubbly, about 8 seconds.

APPLE-CRANBERRY
UPSIDE-DOWN CAKE

Lemon-Blueberry Pound Cake

HANDS-ON PREP 20 MIN   COOK 1 HR 10 MIN   SERVES 12

2   cups all-purpose flour
1   tablespoon grated lemon zest
    (about 2 lemons)
1   teaspoon baking powder
½   teaspoon baking soda
½   teaspoon salt
6   tablespoons unsalted butter, softened
1¼ cups sugar
1   teaspoon vanilla extract

⅔   cup fat-free egg substitute
½   cup reduced-fat sour cream, at room
    temperature
1   cup fresh or frozen blueberries

1 Preheat the oven to 350°F. Spray a 4½ x 8½-inch loaf pan with nonstick spray.

2 Whisk together the flour, lemon zest, baking powder, baking soda, and salt in a medium bowl; set aside.
With an electric mixer on medium speed, beat the butter until creamy, about 1 minute. Add the sugar and vanilla
and beat until light and fluffy, about 4 minutes. Reduce the speed to low. Gradually beat in the egg substitute.
Alternately add the flour mixture and sour cream, beginning and ending with the flour mixture and beating just
until blended. Gently fold in the blueberries.

3 Scrape the batter into the pan; spread evenly. Bake until a toothpick inserted into the center comes out clean,
about 1 hour 10 minutes. Let cool in the pan on a rack 10 minutes. Remove the cake from the pan and let cool
completely on the rack.

PER SERVING (1/12 cake): 236 Cal, 7 g Fat, 4 g Sat Fat, 0 g Trans Fat, 19 mg Chol, 223 mg Sod, 39 g Carb, 1 g Fib,
4 g Prot, 44 mg Calc. **POINTS** value: **5.**

Food Note   It's important to beat the butter, sugar, and vanilla until light and fluffy. It only takes about
4 minutes, and it results in a wonderfully light, fine-textured crumb. Toast any leftover slices for a delicious
afternoon treat.

Cherry-Almond Crumb Cake

HANDS-ON PREP 25 MIN   COOK 35 MIN   SERVES 16

CRUMB TOPPING

2   tablespoons cake flour

2   tablespoons packed light brown sugar

2   tablespoons sliced almonds

1   tablespoon canola oil

½   teaspoon cinnamon

CAKE

2   cups cake flour

2   teaspoons baking powder

½   teaspoon salt

½   cup almond paste (from 7-ounce package)

½   cup granulated sugar

¾   cup low-fat (1%) milk

¼   cup canola oil

1   large egg

1   egg white

½   teaspoon almond extract

¾   cup dried tart cherries

1 Preheat the oven to 350°F. Spray a 9-inch round baking pan with nonstick spray. Line the bottom with a wax-paper round; spray with nonstick spray.

2 To make the crumb topping, stir together the topping ingredients in a small bowl until moistened; set aside.

3 To make the cake, whisk together the cake flour, baking powder, and salt in a medium bowl; set aside. With an electric mixer on medium speed, beat the almond paste and granulated sugar in a large bowl until smooth, about 1 minute. Reduce the speed to low. Add the milk, oil, egg, egg white, and almond extract and beat until smooth. Beat in the flour mixture and cherries just until blended.

4 Pour the batter into the pan; sprinkle evenly with the crumb topping. Bake until a toothpick inserted into the center comes out clean and the topping is golden, about 35 minutes. Let cool in the pan on a rack 10 minutes. Invert the cake onto the rack; remove the wax paper. Let cool completely.

PER SERVING (1/16 of cake): 203 Cal, 7 g Fat, 1 g Sat Fat, 0 g Trans Fat, 14 mg Chol, 149 mg Sod, 32 g Carb, 2 g Fib, 4 g Prot, 69 mg Calc. ***POINTS*** value: **4.**

Food Note   Almond paste is not to be confused with marzipan: Almond paste is a mixture of blanched ground almonds and sugar, while marzipan contains ground almonds, egg whites, and a larger amount of sugar. Almond paste is often used to add rich almond flavor and moisture to baked goods; marzipan is often tinted with food coloring and shaped into fruits and other decorative shapes during the holidays. Leftover almond paste can be stored, tightly wrapped in plastic wrap, in the refrigerator up to 3 weeks or in the freezer up to 3 months.

Citrus-Glazed Orange-Poppy Seed Cake

HANDS-ON PREP 15 MIN   COOK 35 MIN   SERVES 12

CAKE

2   cups cake flour

2   teaspoons poppy seeds

2   teaspoons baking powder

½   teaspoon baking soda

½   teaspoon salt

¾   cup sugar

3   tablespoons canola oil

1   large egg

½   cup low-fat (1%) milk

¼   cup vanilla fat-free yogurt

1   tablespoon grated orange zest
     (about 1 orange)

GLAZE

3   tablespoons sugar

3   tablespoons fresh orange juice

1   teaspoon fresh lemon juice

1 Preheat the oven to 350°F. Spray an 8-inch round baking pan with nonstick spray. Line with a wax-paper round; spray with nonstick spray.

2 To make the cake, whisk together the flour, poppy seeds, baking powder, baking soda, and salt in a medium bowl; set aside. With an electric mixer on medium speed, beat the sugar, oil, and egg in a large bowl until thickened, about 2 minutes. Reduce the speed to low. Add the milk, yogurt, and orange zest and beat until blended. Add the flour mixture and beat just until blended.

3 Pour the batter into the pan. Bake until a toothpick inserted into the center comes out clean, 35–40 minutes. Let cool in the pan on a rack 10 minutes. Run a thin knife around the cake to loosen it from the pan. Invert onto the rack; remove the wax paper. Let cool.

4 Meanwhile, to make the glaze, combine the glaze ingredients in a small saucepan; bring to a boil over medium-high heat. Boil, stirring occasionally, until the mixture begins to thicken, about 3 minutes. Remove the saucepan from the heat. With a wooden skewer, poke holes all over the top of the cake. Brush the hot glaze over the top of the warm cake, allowing the glaze to seep in before brushing with more glaze.

PER SERVING (¹⁄₁₂ of cake): 193 Cal, 4 g Fat, 1 g Sat Fat, 0 g Trans Fat, 18 mg Chol, 245 mg Sod, 36 g Carb, 1 g Fib, 3 g Prot, 79 mg Calc. **POINTS** value: **4.**

Good Idea Poppy seeds, sesame seeds, and nuts contain a good amount of fat, so they easily turn rancid, especially in warm weather. They are best stored in the refrigerator or freezer.

Pineapple Chiffon Cake with Coconut-Rum Glaze

HANDS-ON PREP 20 MIN   COOK 1 HR   SERVES 16

CAKE

2¼ cups cake flour

1½ cups granulated sugar

1   teaspoon baking powder

¾ teaspoon salt

1   (8-ounce) can crushed pineapple

4   egg yolks

⅓ cup canola oil

1   tablespoon grated lime zest (about 2 limes)

8   egg whites, at room temperature

¾ teaspoon cream of tartar

GLAZE

1   cup confectioners' sugar

1   teaspoon coconut extract

½ teaspoon rum extract

1 Preheat the oven to 350°F.

2 To make the cake, whisk together the cake flour, 1 cup of the granulated sugar, the baking powder, and salt in a medium bowl; set aside. Drain the pineapple; reserve 1 tablespoon of the juice. Whisk together the pineapple, egg yolks, oil, and lime zest in a large bowl. Add the flour mixture to the pineapple mixture; stir just until blended.

3 With an electric mixer on medium speed, beat the egg whites and cream of tartar in a large bowl until soft peaks form. Add the remaining ½ cup of granulated sugar, 1 tablespoon at a time, beating until stiff, glossy peaks form. With a rubber spatula, stir about one-fourth of the beaten egg whites into the flour mixture to lighten it. Gently fold in the remaining whites just until no streaks of white remain.

4 Scrape the batter into an ungreased 10-inch tube pan; spread evenly. Bake until the cake is golden brown and springs back when lightly pressed, about 1 hour. Invert the pan onto its legs or the neck of a bottle; let cool completely. Run a thin knife around the cake to loosen it from the side and center tube of the pan. Remove the cake from the pan and place, bottom side up, on a serving plate.

5 To make the glaze, whisk together the confectioners' sugar, the reserved pineapple juice, the coconut extract, and rum extract in a small bowl until smooth. Drizzle over the cake; let stand until set, about 20 minutes.

PER SERVING (1/16 of cake): 242 Cal, 6 g Fat, 1 g Sat Fat, 0 g Trans Fat, 51 mg Chol, 171 mg Sod, 44 g Carb, 1 g Fib, 4 g Prot, 29 mg Calc. *POINTS* value: *5.*

Boston Cream Pie

HANDS-ON PREP 25 MIN   COOK 40 MIN   SERVES 12

CUSTARD

¼ cup sugar

3 tablespoons cornstarch

¼ teaspoon salt

1 cup low-fat (1%) milk

1 large egg

½ teaspoon vanilla extract

CAKE

1½ cups cake flour

1½ teaspoons baking powder

¼ teaspoon salt

¾ cup low-fat (1%) milk

½ cup + 3 tablespoons sugar

3 tablespoons canola oil

1 large egg

1 tablespoon grated orange zest
   (about 1 orange)

3 egg whites

GLAZE

2 ounces semisweet chocolate, chopped

3 tablespoons fat-free half-and-half

1 tablespoon dark corn syrup

1 To make the custard, whisk together the sugar, cornstarch, and salt in a heavy medium saucepan. Whisk in milk and egg and set over medium heat. Cook, stirring, until the custard boils. Cook, stirring, until thickened. Remove from the heat; stir in the vanilla. Press plastic wrap directly onto the surface of the custard; refrigerate.

2 Preheat the oven to 350°F. Spray a 9-inch round baking pan with nonstick spray. Line with a wax-paper round; spray with nonstick spray.

3 To make the cake, whisk together the flour, baking powder, and salt in a medium bowl. Whisk together the milk, ½ cup of the sugar, the oil, egg, and orange zest in a large bowl; stir in the flour mixture just until blended. With an electric mixer on medium speed, beat the egg whites in a medium bowl until soft peaks form. Add the remaining 3 tablespoons of sugar, 1 tablespoon at a time, beating just until firm peaks form. With a rubber spatula, gently fold the beaten whites into the batter until no streaks of white remain. Pour the batter into the pan. Bake until a toothpick inserted into the center comes out clean, about 35 minutes. Let cool completely in the pan on a rack. Run a knife around the cake to loosen it from the pan. Invert.

4 To make the glaze, combine the glaze ingredients in a microwavable bowl. Microwave on High until the chocolate is melted, about 30 seconds. Stir until smooth; let cool.

5 Split the cake layer in half with a long serrated knife. Place the bottom layer, cut side up, on a serving plate. Spread the custard evenly over the layer, leaving a ½-inch border. Place the remaining layer on top, rounded side up. Spoon the chocolate glaze over the top, allowing it to drip down the side of the cake. Refrigerate until set.

PER SERVING (1/12 of cake): 218 Cal, 6 g Fat, 2 g Sat Fat, 0 g Trans Fat, 20 mg Chol, 202 mg Sod, 38 g Carb, 1 g Fib, 4 g Prot, 88 mg Calc. **POINTS** value: **5.**

BOSTON CREAM PIE

Strawberries and Cream Cake Roll

HANDS-ON PREP 25 MIN   COOK 10 MIN   SERVES 8

4   tablespoons confectioners' sugar
6   egg whites, at room temperature
¾   cup granulated sugar
3   egg yolks
1   tablespoon grated orange zest
    (about 1 orange)
3   tablespoons fresh orange juice
1   teaspoon vanilla extract

½   cup all-purpose flour
⅓   cup strawberry jam
1   cup sliced strawberries
1½ cups thawed frozen fat-free whipped topping

1 Preheat the oven to 350°F. Spray a 10½ x 15½ x 1-inch jelly-roll pan with nonstick spray. Line with wax paper; spray with nonstick spray. Dust a clean kitchen towel with 1 tablespoon of the confectioners' sugar; set aside.

2 With an electric mixer on high speed, beat the egg whites in a large bowl until soft peaks form. Add ¼ cup of the granulated sugar, 1 tablespoon at a time, beating until stiff, glossy peaks form. Set aside. In a medium bowl, with the mixer on high speed (no need to clean the beaters), beat the egg yolks until pale and thickened, about 4 minutes. Gradually add the remaining ½ cup of granulated sugar, beating until a ribbon forms when the beaters are lifted. Reduce the speed to low. Beat in the orange zest and juice and vanilla until blended. With a rubber spatula, gradually stir in the flour until well blended. Gently fold the beaten whites into the egg yolk mixture just until no streaks of white remain.

3 Pour the batter into the pan; spread evenly. Bake until the cake is golden and springs back when lightly pressed, 10–13 minutes. Run a thin knife around the cake to loosen it from the pan; invert onto the sugar-dusted towel; remove the wax paper. While the cake is still warm and starting with a short side, roll up the cake with the towel. Place on a rack and let cool completely.

4 Unroll the cake and remove the towel. With a narrow metal spatula, spread the jam over the cake. Sprinkle evenly with the strawberries, then spread evenly with the whipped topping. Reroll the cake; place, seam side down, on a serving plate. Dust with the remaining 3 tablespoons of confectioners' sugar. Wearing oven mitts, heat a long metal skewer on the stovetop until very hot, about 10 seconds. Drag the hot skewer through the sugar, on the diagonal, to make a crosshatch pattern. Reheat the skewer, being sure to wipe it clean each time.

PER SERVING (⅛ of cake): 216 Cal, 2 g Fat, 1 g Sat Fat, 0 g Trans Fat, 77 mg Chol, 53 mg Sod, 45 g Carb, 1 g Fib, 5 g Prot, 20 mg Calc. **POINTS** value: **4.**

Double Chocolate Angel Food Cake with Strawberries

HANDS-ON PREP 35 MIN   COOK 35 MIN   SERVES 12

1½ cups cake flour

¾ cup unsweetened cocoa powder

½ teaspoon salt

2 ounces bittersweet or semisweet chocolate, coarsely grated

12 egg whites, at room temperature

1 teaspoon cream of tartar

1½ cups sugar

1 teaspoon vanilla extract

2 (1-pound) containers strawberries

1½ cups thawed frozen fat-free whipped topping

1 Place an oven rack in the lower third of the oven and preheat the oven to 375°F.

2 Sift together the flour, ½ cup of the cocoa, and the salt into a medium bowl. Stir in the chocolate; set aside. With an electric mixer on medium speed, beat the egg whites and cream of tartar until soft peaks form. Add the sugar, 2 tablespoons at a time, beating until stiff, glossy peaks form. Beat in the vanilla.

3 Sift the cocoa mixture, one-third at a time, over the beaten egg whites, gently folding it in with a rubber spatula just until the cocoa is no longer visible. (Be careful not to overmix.)

4 Scrape the batter into an ungreased 10-inch tube pan; spread evenly. Bake until the cake springs back when lightly pressed, 35–40 minutes. Invert the pan onto its legs or the neck of a bottle and let cool completely. Run a thin knife around the edge of the cake to loosen it from the side and center tube of the pan. Remove the cake from the pan and put on a serving plate; dust with the remaining ¼ cup of cocoa. Serve the strawberries and whipped topping alongside.

PER SERVING (1/12 of cake, 3 strawberries, and 2 tablespoons whipping topping): 248 Cal, 3 g Fat, 2 g Sat Fat, 0 g Trans Fat, 0 mg Chol, 159 mg Sod, 53 g Carb, 4 g Fib, 7 g Prot, 26 mg Calc. *POINTS* value: **4.**

Food Note   Some tube pans have three small "feet" set along the edge of the pan. When the cake pan is inverted, the pan rests on its feet allowing the cake to cool. If your pan does not have feet, use a narrow-necked bottle, such as a wine bottle or an inverted metal funnel.

Chocolate-Glazed Chocolate Bundt Cake

HANDS-ON PREP 20 MIN   COOK 45 MIN   SERVES 24

CAKE

2 cups all-purpose flour

1¼ cups granulated sugar

2 teaspoons baking powder

½ teaspoon baking soda

½ teaspoon salt

½ cup unsweetened cocoa powder

1 ounce bittersweet or semisweet chocolate, finely chopped

1 tablespoon instant espresso powder

½ cup boiling water

1 tablespoon vanilla extract

1 cup low-fat buttermilk

⅓ cup canola oil

1 large egg

1 egg white

¾ cup semisweet chocolate chips

GLAZE

½ cup confectioners' sugar

2 ounces semisweet chocolate, melted

3 tablespoons fat-free half-and-half

1 Preheat the oven to 325°F. Spray a 10-inch Bundt pan with nonstick spray.

2 To make the cake, whisk together the flour, granulated sugar, baking powder, baking soda, and salt in a medium bowl; set aside. Combine the cocoa, chopped chocolate, and espresso powder in a small bowl. Pour the boiling water over the cocoa mixture, stirring until the chocolate is melted and the mixture is smooth. Stir in the vanilla. Whisk together the buttermilk, oil, egg, and egg white in a large bowl; stir in the cocoa mixture until blended. Gradually add the flour mixture, stirring just until blended. Stir in the chocolate chips.

3 Pour the mixture into the pan. Bake until a toothpick inserted into the center comes out clean, 45–50 minutes. Let cool in the pan on a rack 10 minutes. Remove the cake from the pan and let cool completely on the rack.

4 To make the glaze, whisk together the glaze ingredients in a small bowl until smooth. Let stand until cool and thickened, about 15 minutes. Place the cake on a serving plate. Pour the glaze over, allowing it to drip down the side of the cake. Let stand until set, about 10 minutes.

PER SERVING (¹⁄₂₄ of cake): 172 Cal, 6 g Fat, 2 g Sat Fat, 0 g Trans Fat, 9 mg Chol, 136 mg Sod, 28 g Carb, 1 g Fib, 3 g Prot, 45 mg Calc. *POINTS* value: *4.*

Good Idea   To dress up the cake with long and elegant chocolate curls, run a vegetable peeler across a bar of room-temperature chocolate to make curls.

CHOCOLATE-GLAZED
CHOCOLATE BUNDT CAKE

Chocolate-Raspberry Soufflé Cakes

HANDS-ON PREP 20 MIN   COOK 30 MIN   SERVES 6

- 2 tablespoons + ¾ cup sugar
- 1½ cups fresh raspberries
- 2 tablespoons cornstarch
- ¼ teaspoon salt
- 1 cup low-fat (1%) milk
- 3 ounces bittersweet or semisweet chocolate, chopped
- 1 teaspoon vanilla extract
- ½ teaspoon almond extract
- 2 egg yolks
- 4 egg whites, at room temperature
- ½ teaspoon cream of tartar
- Confectioners' sugar (optional)

1 Preheat the oven to 400°F. Spray six 6-ounce baking dishes or ramekins with nonstick spray.

2 Sprinkle 2 tablespoons of the sugar into a baking dish, turning to coat the bottom and side evenly. Pour the excess sugar into a second baking dish to coat. Repeat with the remaining baking dishes. Divide the raspberries evenly among the dishes; set aside.

3 Whisk together ½ cup of the sugar, the cornstarch, and salt in a medium saucepan. Whisk in the milk and set over medium heat. Cook, stirring constantly, until the mixture thickens and begins to boil, 3–4 minutes. Put the chocolate in a large bowl. Pour the milk mixture over the chocolate, stirring until the chocolate melts and the mixture is smooth. Stir in the vanilla and almond extracts. Let cool slightly, then beat in the egg yolks, one at a time, until well blended; set aside.

4 With an electric mixer on medium speed, beat the egg whites and cream of tartar in a large bowl until soft peaks form. Add the remaining ¼ cup of sugar, 1 tablespoon at a time, beating until stiff, glossy peaks form. With a rubber spatula, stir about one-fourth of the beaten egg whites into the chocolate mixture to lighten it. Gently fold in the remaining egg whites just until no streaks of white remain.

5 Spoon the chocolate mixture into the baking dishes, filling each about three-fourths full. Place the dishes in a large roasting pan. Put the pan in the oven; add enough hot water to come halfway up the sides of the dishes. Bake until puffed and golden, 20–25 minutes. Wearing oven mitts or with sturdy tongs, remove the soufflé cakes from the water bath. Lightly dust with confectioners' sugar (if using) and serve at once.

PER SERVING (1 soufflé cake): 259 Cal, 6 g Fat, 3 g Sat Fat, 0 g Trans Fat, 70 mg Chol, 158 mg Sod, 47 g Carb, 3 g Fib, 6 g Prot, 70 mg Calc. **POINTS** value: **5.**

Classic New York-Style Cheesecake

HANDS-ON PREP 15 MIN   COOK 55 MIN   SERVES 24

CRUST

10 reduced-fat graham crackers, crushed to crumbs (about 1½ cups)

1 tablespoon light corn syrup

1 tablespoon unsalted butter, melted

TOPPING

2 cups fat-free sour cream

¼ cup sugar

1 teaspoon vanilla extract

CAKE

4 (8-ounce) packages light cream cheese (Neufchâtel), softened

1¼ cups sugar

2 large eggs

2 egg whites

1 tablespoon grated lemon zest (about 2 lemons)

1 tablespoon fresh lemon juice

1 teaspoon vanilla extract

1 Preheat the oven to 350°F. Spray a 10-inch springform pan with nonstick spray.

2 To make the crust, combine the crust ingredients in a small bowl until moistened. Press the crumb mixture firmly onto the bottom of the pan; refrigerate.

3 To make the topping, whisk together the topping ingredients in a medium bowl; cover and refrigerate.

4 To make the cake, with an electric mixer on medium speed, beat the cream cheese in a large bowl until very smooth, about 3 minutes. Gradually add the sugar, beating until fluffy, about 2 minutes. Beat in the eggs, one at a time, until well blended. Beat in the egg whites, lemon zest and juice, and vanilla until blended.

5 Pour the batter over the crust. Bake until the edge of the cheesecake is set and the center jiggles slightly, 55–60 minutes. Let cool in the pan on a rack 15 minutes. Spoon the sour cream topping over the cake; spread evenly with a narrow metal spatula. Cover and refrigerate at least 8 hours or up to 2 days.

PER SERVING (1/24 of cake): 201 Cal, 10 g Fat, 6 g Sat Fat, 1 g Trans Fat, 49 mg Chol, 229 mg Sod, 22 g Carb, 0 g Fib, 6 g Prot, 63 mg Calc. **POINTS** value: **5.**

How We Did it   To crush the graham crackers, place them in a large zip-close plastic bag, squeeze out the air, and seal the bag. Use a rolling pin or the bottom of a heavy saucepan to turn the crackers into fine crumbs.

PEANUT BUTTER AND JELLY CUPCAKES

Peanut Butter and Jelly Cupcakes

HANDS-ON PREP 20 MIN   COOK 25 MIN   SERVES 24

FROSTING

- ½ cup light cream cheese (Neufchâtel), softened
- ¼ cup reduced-fat creamy peanut butter
- ¼ cup confectioners' sugar

CUPCAKES

- 1 cup cake flour
- 1 cup granulated sugar
- ½ cup unsweetened cocoa powder
- 1 teaspoon baking powder
- ¼ teaspoon baking soda
- ¼ teaspoon salt
- ½ cup low-fat buttermilk
- ⅓ cup canola oil
- 1 large egg
- 1 egg white
- 1 teaspoon vanilla extract
- 1 ounce semisweet chocolate, melted and cooled
- ½ cup seedless raspberry jam
- ¼ cup unsalted roasted peanuts, chopped

1 Preheat the oven to 350°F. Spray a 24-cup mini-muffin pan with nonstick spray.

2 To make the frosting, with an electric mixer on low speed, beat the frosting ingredients in a small bowl until smooth, about 2 minutes. Cover with plastic wrap; set aside.

3 To make the cupcakes, whisk together the cake flour, granulated sugar, cocoa, baking powder, baking soda, and salt in a medium bowl. Whisk together the buttermilk, oil, egg, egg white, and vanilla in a large bowl. Whisk in the melted chocolate. Add the flour mixture, stirring just until blended.

4 Fill each muffin cup two-thirds full with the batter. Bake until a toothpick inserted into the center comes out clean, about 25 minutes. Let cool in the pan on a rack 10 minutes. Remove the cupcakes from the pan and let cool completely on the rack.

5 Fit a small pastry bag with a plain medium tip and fill with the jam. Carefully insert the pastry tip into the top of a cupcake. Pipe in about 1 of teaspoon jam. Repeat with the remaining cupcakes and jam. With a small metal spatula, spread the frosting over the tops of the cupcakes; sprinkle with the peanuts.

PER SERVING (1 cupcake): 157 Cal, 7 g Fat, 2 g Sat Fat, 0 g Trans Fat, 13 mg Chol, 107 mg Sod, 22 g Carb, 1 g Fib, 3 g Prot, 29 mg Calc. **POINTS** value: **4.**

Good Idea   To make ahead, store the unfrosted cupcakes in an airtight container at room temperature up to 3 days or freeze in a zip-close plastic bag up to 3 weeks. Allow the frozen cupcakes to come to room temperature before frosting.

Pies, Tarts & More

Chapter 2

Pastry Dough for Single Crust

HANDS-ON PREP 20 MIN   **SERVES** 8

1   **cup all-purpose flour**
1   **tablespoon confectioners' sugar**
½   **teaspoon salt**
3   **tablespoons canola oil**
1   **tablespoon cold unsalted butter, cut into pieces**
1   **teaspoon apple-cider vinegar**
About 4 tablespoons ice water

1 Combine the flour, confectioners' sugar, and salt in a medium bowl. With a pastry blender or 2 knives used scissor-fashion, cut in the oil and butter until the mixture resembles coarse crumbs. Combine the water and vinegar in a small bowl. Gradually add to the flour mixture, tossing lightly with a fork until the pastry is just moist enough to hold together.

2 Shape the dough into a disk. Wrap in plastic wrap and refrigerate until chilled, at least 30 minutes or up to 1 day.

PER SERVING (⅛ of dough): 120 Cal, 8 g Fat, 2 g Sat Fat, 0 g Trans Fat, 5 mg Chol, 146 mg Sod, 14 g Carb, 0 g Fib, 2 g Prot, 3 mg Calc. **POINTS** value: **3.**

Pastry Dough for Double Crust

Double the ingredients for the Pastry Dough for Single Crust; proceed as directed through step 1. Divide the dough in half. Shape each piece of dough into a disk. Wrap each disk in plastic wrap and refrigerate until chilled, at least 30 minutes or up to 1 day.

Food Processor Method (for single and double crust)

Put the flour, confectioners' sugar, and salt in a food processor; pulse until blended. Add the oil and butter; pulse until the mixture resembles coarse crumbs. Combine the water and vinegar in a small bowl. Pour through the feed tube, pulsing just until a dough forms. Proceed as directed.

French Apple Tarts

HANDS-ON PREP 30 MIN   **COOK** 30 MIN   **SERVES** 8

Pastry Dough for Single Crust (page 34)

FILLING

2   large Granny Smith apples (about 1 pound),
     peeled, halved, cored, and thinly sliced
2   tablespoons unsalted butter, melted
4   teaspoons granulated sugar
4   teaspoons confectioners' sugar

1 Preheat the oven to 425°F. Line a large baking sheet with foil; spray with nonstick spray.

2 Divide the dough into 4 equal pieces. Shape each piece into a disk. On a lightly floured surface, roll out each disk of dough to a 6-inch round; place on the baking sheet. Arrange one-fourth of the apple slices in a concentric circle of overlapping slices on each dough round, leaving a ¼-inch border. Brush the apples with the melted butter and sprinkle with the granulated sugar. Bake until the apples are tender and golden, about 30 minutes.

3 Preheat the broiler.

4 Dust the confectioners' sugar evenly over the apples. Broil 4 inches from the heat until the apples begin to bubble and lightly char around the edges, 3–4 minutes. Cut each tart in half and serve hot, warm, or at room temperature.

PER SERVING (½ tart): 181 Cal, 10 g Fat, 3 g Sat Fat, 0 g Trans Fat, 11 mg Chol, 149 mg Sod, 22 g Carb, 1 g Fib, 2 g Prot, 7 mg Calc. **POINTS** value: **4.**

Food Note   These tasty little tarts are also delicious with firm-ripe stone fruits, such as peaches, nectarines, apricots, or plums. If you like, instead of dusting the tarts with confectioners' sugar, brush them with a little melted apricot jam before placing under the broiler.

Old-Fashioned Apple Crumb Pie

HANDS-ON PREP 30 MIN   COOK 55 MIN   SERVES 10

Pastry Dough for Single Crust (page 34)

FILLING

- ⅓ cup sugar
- 1 teaspoon cinnamon
- ¼ teaspoon salt
- 4 large Golden Delicious apples (about 1½ pounds), peeled, halved, cored, and cut into ¼-inch-thick slices
- 1 tablespoon grated lemon zest (about 2 lemons)
- 1 tablespoon fresh lemon juice

CRUMB TOPPING

- ¼ cup all-purpose flour
- ¼ cup whole-wheat pastry flour
- 2 tablespoons rolled (old-fashioned) oats
- 2 tablespoons canola oil
- 1 tablespoon sugar
- ½ teaspoon cinnamon

Thawed frozen fat-free whipped topping, for serving (optional)

1 Preheat the oven to 375°F.

2 On a lightly floured surface, roll out the pastry dough to a 12-inch round; ease into a 9-inch pie plate, pressing it against the side of the pie plate. Leaving a 1-inch border, trim off any excess dough. Crimp the edge to form a decorative rim; set aside.

3 To make the filling, combine the sugar, cinnamon, and salt in a large bowl. Add the apples and lemon zest and juice; toss to mix well. Spoon into the pie shell.

4 To make the topping, using a fork, stir together the topping ingredients in a medium bowl until well blended. Squeeze the mixture together to form a loose ball, then break into small pieces and sprinkle evenly over the filling. Bake until the filling is bubbly and the topping is golden, about 55 minutes. Loosely cover the pie with a piece of foil during the last 15 minutes to prevent overbrowning, if necessary. Let cool on a rack until warm before serving. Serve with whipped topping (if using).

PER SERVING (¹⁄₁₀ of pie without whipped topping): 214 Cal, 8 g Fat, 1 g Sat Fat, 0 g Trans Fat, 3 mg Chol, 178 mg Sod, 34 g Carb, 2 g Fib, 2 g Prot, 14 mg Calc. **POINTS** value: **5.**

Try It Golden Delicious apples make a pie filling that is deliciously sweet. If you like your apple pie with more of a sweet-tart flavor, use Granny Smiths or a combination of apples.

OLD-FASHIONED
APPLE CRUMB PIE

Fresh Apricot Tart

HANDS-ON PREP 45 MIN   COOK 1 HR   SERVES 8

CRUST

1   cup all-purpose flour
¼   cup sliced blanched almonds
1   tablespoon confectioners' sugar
½   teaspoon salt
3   tablespoons canola oil
1   tablespoon unsalted butter, cut into pieces
About 4 tablespoons ice water
1   teaspoon apple-cider vinegar

FILLING

½   cup unsweetened chunky-style applesauce
6   ripe apricots (about ¾ pound), halved
    and pitted
¼   cup apricot jam, melted
2   tablespoons chopped pistachio nuts

1 Preheat the oven to 400°F.

2 To make the crust, put the flour, almonds, confectioners' sugar, and salt in a food processor; pulse until the almonds are finely ground. Add the oil and butter; pulse until the mixture resembles coarse crumbs. Combine the water and vinegar in a small bowl. Pour through the feed tube, pulsing just until the dough comes together. Shape into a disk. On a lightly floured surface, roll out the dough to a 12-inch round; ease into a 9-inch removable bottom tart pan, pressing the dough against the side of the pan. Prick the dough with a fork. Roll a rolling pin over the rim of the pan to cut off the overhanging dough.

3 Line the tart shell with a piece of foil; fill with dried beans or rice. Bake until set, about 20 minutes; remove the foil with the beans. Bake until golden, 10–12 minutes longer. Place the tart pan on a rack and let cool about 10 minutes.

4 Spread the applesauce over the bottom of the tart shell. Arrange the apricots, cut side up, on top of the applesauce. Brush with the jam, then sprinkle with the pistachios. Bake until the apricots are tender and lightly browned, about 25 minutes. Let cool on a rack about 20 minutes. Remove the side of the pan and cut the tart into wedges.

PER SERVING (⅛ of tart): 195 Cal, 9 g Fat, 2 g Sat Fat, 0 g Trans Fat, 4 mg Chol, 153 mg Sod, 26 g Carb, 2 g Fib, 3 g Prot, 18 mg Calc. *POINTS* value: **4.**

Plan Ahead   The dough is ready to be rolled out as soon as it is prepared, but you can get a head start by wrapping it in plastic wrap and refrigerating up to 1 day, if you like.

Country Blueberry Pie

HANDS-ON PREP 20 MIN   COOK 45 MIN   SERVES 12

¾   cup + 1 tablespoon sugar
3   tablespoons cornstarch
1   teaspoon cinnamon
⅛   teaspoon salt
4   cups blueberries (about 2 pints)
1   tablespoon grated lemon zest
     (about 2 lemons)
1   tablespoon fresh lemon juice
Pastry Dough for Double Crust (page 34)
1   egg white, lightly beaten
1   teaspoon water

1 Preheat the oven to 425°F.

2 To make the filling, combine ¾ cup of the sugar, the cornstarch, cinnamon, and salt in a large bowl. Add the blueberries and lemon zest and juice; toss to mix well.

3 On a lightly floured surface, roll out 1 disk of dough to a 12-inch round; ease into a 9-inch pie plate, pressing it against the side of the pie plate. Spoon the blueberry mixture into the pie shell.

4 Roll out the second disk of dough to a 12-inch round; place over the filling. Crimp the dough edges together to form a decorative rim. Brush the top of the pie with the beaten egg white and sprinkle with the remaining 1 tablespoon of sugar. With a knife, make several 1-inch slits in the top of the pie.

5 Place the pie on a baking sheet to catch any drips. Bake 20 minutes; reduce the temperature to 375°F. Bake until the crust is golden and the filling is bubbly, about 25 minutes. Let cool on a rack about 1 hour before serving.

PER SERVING (¹⁄₁₂ of pie): 248 Cal, 9 g Fat, 2 g Sat Fat, 0 g Trans Fat, 5 mg Chol, 227 mg Sod, 40 g Carb, 2 g Fib, 3 g Prot, 10 mg Calc. **POINTS** value: **5.**

Good Idea   A small scoop of vanilla fat-free frozen yogurt is the perfect accompaniment for this summertime classic (¼ cup scoop of fat-free frozen yogurt will increase the **POINTS** value by **1).**

CHOCOLATE-HAZELNUT
MERINGUE PIE

Chocolate-Hazelnut Meringue Pie

HANDS-ON PREP 30 MIN   COOK 30 MIN   SERVES 12

FILLING

½ cup sugar

¼ cup all-purpose flour

¼ teaspoon salt

1½ cups low-fat (1%) milk

1 large egg

¼ cup semisweet chocolate chips

2 tablespoons hazelnut-flavored syrup or liqueur

1 (6-ounce) prepared chocolate cookie crust

MERINGUE TOPPING

4 egg whites, at room temperature

½ teaspoon cream of tartar

½ cup sugar

2 tablespoons hazelnut-flavored syrup or liqueur

1 Preheat the oven to 375°F.

2 To make the filling, whisk together the sugar, flour, and salt in a medium saucepan. Whisk in the milk and egg, then set over medium-high heat. Cook, stirring constantly, until the mixture thickens and boils, about 4 minutes; let boil 1 minute. Remove the saucepan from the heat; whisk in the chocolate chips and syrup until the chocolate is melted and the mixture is smooth. Pour into the crust; set aside.

3 To make the meringue, with an electric mixer on medium speed, beat the egg whites and cream of tartar in a large bowl until soft peaks form. Increase the speed to medium-high. Sprinkle in the sugar, 1 tablespoon at a time, beating until stiff, glossy peaks form. Beat in the syrup.

4 Spoon the meringue over the filling, spreading it to the edge of the crust to completely enclose the filling. Bake until the meringue is golden brown, about 15 minutes. Let cool on a rack about 1 hour. Refrigerate at least 3 hours or up to 6 hours. This pie is best eaten the day it is prepared.

PER SERVING (¹⁄₁₂ of pie): 213 Cal, 7 g Fat, 2 g Sat Fat, 2 g Trans Fat, 19 mg Chol, 148 mg Sod, 34 g Carb, 1 g Fib, 4 g Prot, 45 mg Calc. *POINTS* value: *5.*

Try It   Hazelnut syrup can be found in specialty food stores or in the gourmet section of most supermarkets. Use it to flavor coffee or cappuccino or to spoon over low-fat ice cream.

Coconut Cream Pie with Macadamia Crust

HANDS-ON PREP 35 MIN   COOK 12 MIN   SERVES 8

CRUST

15 reduced-fat gingersnap cookies

1 tablespoon + 2 teaspoons canola oil

1 tablespoon chopped macadamia nuts

FILLING

1 envelope unflavored gelatin

¼ cup cold water

¼ cup sugar

3 tablespoons all-purpose flour

1 cup low-fat (1%) milk

½ cup light (reduced-fat) coconut milk

1 large egg

Pinch salt

1 teaspoon coconut extract

½ cup thawed frozen light whipped topping

2 tablespoons flaked sweetened coconut, toasted

1 Preheat the oven to 375°F. Spray a 9-inch pie plate with nonstick spray.

2 To make the crust, put the gingersnaps in a food processor and pulse until finely ground. Add the oil and nuts; process until crumbly. Press the crumb mixture evenly onto the bottom and up the side of the pie plate. Bake until set, 8–10 minutes. Let cool completely on a rack.

3 To make the filling, sprinkle the gelatin over the water in a microwavable cup. Let stand until softened, about 5 minutes. Microwave on High until the gelatin is completely dissolved, about 15 seconds; set aside.

4 Whisk together the sugar and flour in a medium saucepan. Whisk in the milk, coconut milk, egg, and salt and set over medium-high heat. Cook, stirring constantly, until the mixture thickens, about 4 minutes (do not let boil). Remove the saucepan from the heat. Stir in the gelatin mixture and coconut extract. Pour into a medium bowl; refrigerate until the filling begins to set, about 30 minutes; whisk until smooth and creamy. With a rubber spatula, gently fold in the whipped topping. Pour into the crust and sprinkle with the toasted coconut. Refrigerate until firm, at least 2 hours or up to 6 hours.

PER SERVING (⅛ of pie): 167 Cal, 7 g Fat, 3 g Sat Fat, 0 g Trans Fat, 28 mg Chol, 110 mg Sod, 22 g Carb, 1 g Fib, 4 g Prot, 53 mg Calc. **POINTS** value: **4.**

Express Lane Using a reduced-fat prepared shortbread or graham-cracker crust will save you time in the kitchen.

No-Bake Key Lime Mousse Pie

HANDS-ON PREP 25 MIN   COOK 6 MIN   SERVES 8

½ cup + 2 tablespoons sugar

2 large eggs

1 egg yolk

1 teaspoon cornstarch

1 envelope unflavored gelatin

½ cup fresh lime juice (about 4 limes)

1 tablespoon grated lime zest (about 2 limes)

6 tablespoons warm water

3 tablespoons powdered egg whites

¼ teaspoon cream of tartar

½ cup plain reduced-fat (2%) Greek-style yogurt

1 (6-ounce) prepared reduced-fat graham-cracker crust

1 small lime, thinly sliced

1 To make the filling, whisk together ½ cup of the sugar, the eggs, egg yolk, and cornstarch in a large bowl until the sugar is dissolved and the mixture is pale.

2 Sprinkle the gelatin over the lime juice in a small saucepan. Let stand until the gelatin is softened, about 5 minutes. Heat over medium heat, stirring occasionally, until the gelatin is completely dissolved, about 2 minutes. Stir in the sugar mixture and lime zest; cook, stirring occasionally, until thickened, about 4 minutes (do not let boil). Immediately pour into a medium bowl; refrigerate until the filling begins to set, about 30 minutes.

3 Stir together the warm water, powdered egg whites, cream of tartar, and the remaining 2 tablespoons of sugar in a medium bowl until the egg white powder is completely dissolved, about 2 minutes. With an electric mixer on medium speed, beat the egg white mixture until stiff, glossy peaks form.

4 Whisk the lime juice mixture until smooth and creamy. With a rubber spatula, gently fold in the yogurt then the beaten egg whites just until no streaks of white remain. Spoon into the crust; spread evenly. Refrigerate until firm, at least 3 hours or up to overnight. Just before serving, garnish with the lime slices.

PER SERVING (⅛ of pie): 211 Cal, 5 g Fat, 1 g Sat Fat, 1 g Trans Fat, 80 mg Chol, 155 mg Sod, 36 g Carb, 1 g Fib, 6 g Prot, 47 mg Calc. **POINTS** value: **4.**

Play It Safe Dehydrated pasteurized egg whites are a safe alternative to raw egg whites. The whites are heated to kill any bacteria, then turned into a powder. Use egg white powder to prepare mousses, eggnog, chiffon pies, or other dishes that call for raw egg whites. Look for it in the baking aisle of your supermarket and in specialty food stores. Just Whites is one of the most readily available brands.

CRANBERRY-ORANGE
LINZER TART

Cranberry-Orange Linzer Tart

HANDS-ON PREP 40 MIN COOK 1 HR SERVES 12

FILLING

1 (12-ounce) package fresh or frozen cranberries

¾ cup sugar

¾ cup orange juice

¼ cup seedless raspberry fruit spread

2 tablespoons orange-flavored liqueur
   or 1 teaspoon orange extract

1 tablespoon minced peeled fresh ginger

PASTRY DOUGH

1¾ cups all-purpose flour

¼ cup sliced blanched almonds

4 tablespoons sugar

1 tablespoon grated lemon zest (about 2 lemons)

¾ teaspoon cinnamon

½ teaspoon ground allspice

¼ teaspoon salt

6 tablespoons canola oil

2 tablespoons cold unsalted butter, cut
   into pieces

About 5 tablespoons ice water

1 tablespoon low-fat (1%) milk

1 Preheat the oven to 400°F.

2 To make the filling, combine the cranberries, sugar, orange juice, fruit spread, liqueur, and ginger in a medium saucepan and set over medium-high heat; bring to a boil. Cook, stirring occasionally, until the liquid is almost evaporated and the mixture is thick, about 15 minutes. Remove the saucepan from the heat and let cool slightly.

3 Meanwhile, to make the pastry dough, put the flour, almonds, 3 tablespoons of the sugar, the lemon zest, cinnamon, allspice, and salt in a food processor; pulse until blended. Add the oil and butter; pulse until the mixture resembles coarse crumbs. Pour the water through the feed tube, pulsing just until a dough forms. Shape the dough into 2 disks, one slightly larger than the other. On a lightly floured surface, roll out the larger disk into a 12-inch round; ease into a 9-inch removable bottom tart pan, pressing the dough against the side of the pan. Trim the dough edge, leaving a ½-inch overhang; crimp the edge. Roll out the remaining disk of dough to a 7 x 9½-inch rectangle. Cut lengthwise into ½-inch-wide strips.

4 Spread the cranberry mixture evenly in the tart shell. Place half of the dough strips on top of the filling. Place the remaining strips on top, at a right angle to the first set of strips, to form a crisscross pattern, weaving them, if desired. Trim all the strips and press them against the inside of the shell.

5 Brush the pastry strips and rim with the milk and sprinkle with the remaining 1 tablespoon of sugar. Bake until the crust is golden brown and the filling is slightly bubbly, 35–40 minutes. Let cool completely on a rack.

PER SERVING (1/12 of tart): 265 Cal, 10 g Fat, 2 g Sat Fat, 0 g Trans Fat, 5 mg Chol, 53 mg Sod, 41 g Carb, 3 g Fib, 3 g Prot, 19 mg Calc. **POINTS** value: **6.**

Fresh Plum-Raspberry Galettes

HANDS-ON PREP 20 MIN   COOK 30 MIN   SERVES 8

4 ripe medium plums (1¼ pounds), halved, pitted, and cut into 1-inch-thick wedges
1 (6-ounce) container raspberries
⅓ cup + 1 tablespoon sugar
1 teaspoon fresh lemon juice
Pinch salt
Pastry Dough for Single Crust (page 34)
1½ tablespoons sliced almonds

1 Preheat the oven to 425°F. Line a large baking sheet with foil; spray with nonstick spray.

2 To make the filling, combine the plums, raspberries, ⅓ cup of the sugar, the lemon juice, and salt in a medium bowl; set aside.

3 Divide the dough into 4 equal pieces and shape each piece into a disk. On a lightly floured surface, roll out each disk of dough to a 6-inch round. Place the rounds on the baking sheet. Mound one-fourth of the filling on each round, leaving a 2-inch border. Fold the rim of dough over the filling, pleating it as you go around.

4 Sprinkle the fruit filling with the remaining 1 tablespoon of sugar and the almonds. Bake until the plums are tender and the crust is golden, about 30 minutes. Let cool on a rack; cut each galette in half.

PER SERVING (½ galette): 186 Cal, 7 g Fat, 1 g Sat Fat, 0 g Trans Fat, 4 mg Chol, 184 mg Sod, 29 g Carb, 2 g Fib, 2 g Prot, 12 mg Calc. *POINTS* value: *4.*

Plan Ahead Double the recipe for the dough so you have 4 extra disks on hand. Stack them between sheets of wax paper; wrap tightly in plastic wrap and then in foil. They will keep up to 1 month in the freezer.

Raspberry Jam Crostata

HANDS-ON PREP 30 MIN   COOK 35 MIN   SERVES 12

½ cup seedless raspberry jam
1   teaspoon fresh lemon juice
¾ teaspoon almond extract
Pastry Dough for Double Crust (page 34)
3   tablespoons low-fat (1%) milk
2   tablespoons sugar
1   tablespoon sliced unblanched almonds

1 Preheat the oven to 425°F.

2 To make the filling, combine the jam, lemon juice, and almond extract in a small bowl; set aside.

3 On a lightly floured surface, roll out 1 disk of the dough to a 12-inch round; ease into a 9-inch removable bottom tart pan, pressing the dough against the side of the pan. Trim the edge, leaving a ½-inch overhang; crimp the edge. Roll out the remaining disk of dough to an 11-inch square; cut into 1-inch-wide strips.

4 Spread the jam mixture evenly in the tart shell. Place half of the strips over the jam, spacing them evenly. Place the remaining strips on top, at a right angle to the first set of strips, to form a crisscross pattern. Trim all the strips and press them against the inside of the shell.

5 Brush the dough strips and dough rim with the milk; sprinkle with the sugar and almonds. Bake until the crust is browned and the jam is slightly bubbly, about 35 minutes. Let cool completely on a rack.

PER SERVING (¹⁄₁₂ of tart): 209 Cal, 9 g Fat, 2 g Sat Fat, 0 g Trans Fat, 5 mg Chol, 203 mg Sod, 29 g Carb, 1 g Fib, 2 g Prot, 13 mg Calc. **POINTS** value: **5.**

Food Note Crostata (kroh-STAH-tah), from the Latin word *crusta* (crust), is an open-face tart that often has a lattice top; it is enjoyed throughout Italy. Crostatas can be filled with fresh or dried fruit, pastry cream, nuts, custard, ricotta cheese, or chocolate, and all are equally delicious.

Peach-Blueberry Galette

HANDS-ON PREP 30 MIN   **COOK** 45 MIN   **SERVES** 10

¼   **cup packed light brown sugar**

1   **tablespoon all-purpose flour**

¾   **teaspoon cinnamon**

Pinch salt

4   **ripe medium peaches, halved, pitted, and sliced**

1   **cup blueberries**

1   **tablespoon grated lemon zest (about 2 lemons)**

6   **(12 x 17-inch) sheets frozen phyllo dough, thawed**

1   **tablespoon unsalted butter, melted**

1   Preheat the oven to 375°F. Spray a 10-inch pizza pan or large baking sheet with nonstick spray.

2   To make the filling, combine the brown sugar, flour, cinnamon, and salt in a large bowl. Add the peaches, blueberries, and lemon zest; toss to mix well.

3   Lay 1 phyllo sheet in the pan; lightly spray with nonstick spray. Keep the remaining phyllo covered with a damp paper towel and plastic wrap to keep it from drying out. Repeat with the remaining 5 phyllo sheets, placing the corners at different angles and lightly spraying each sheet with nonstick spray. Roll up the edges of the phyllo to form a 1½-inch-wide rim.

4   Spoon the peach mixture evenly on top of the phyllo and drizzle with the melted butter. Bake until the edges of the phyllo are golden brown and the peaches are tender, about 45 minutes. Let cool on a rack about 1 hour before serving.

PER SERVING (¹⁄₁₀ of galette): 102 Cal, 1 g Fat, 1 g Sat Fat, 0 g Trans Fat, 3 mg Chol, 81 mg Sod, 21 g Carb, 1 g Fib, 2 g Prot, 13 mg Calc. ***POINTS*** value: *2.*

How We Did It   For the best results, allow frozen phyllo dough to slowly thaw overnight in the refrigerator. Thawing phyllo at room temperature tends to make the sheets stick together, making them difficult to work with. Phyllo dough dries out quickly, so keep the unused sheets covered with a damp paper towel and then with a sheet of plastic wrap. Any unused phyllo can be tightly wrapped and refrozen for up to 1 month.

Pumpkin-Ginger Chiffon Pie

HANDS-ON PREP 30 MIN   COOK 8 MIN   SERVES 8

1   (15-ounce) can pumpkin puree
¾   cup sugar
1   large egg
1   teaspoon cinnamon
1   teaspoon ground ginger
¼   teaspoon ground cloves
¼   teaspoon salt
2   envelopes unflavored gelatin
1   (12-ounce) can evaporated skim milk

1   cup thawed frozen fat-free whipped topping
1   (6-ounce) prepared reduced-fat graham-cracker crust
2   tablespoons chopped pecans, toasted

1 Whisk together the pumpkin, sugar, egg, cinnamon, ginger, cloves, and salt in a large bowl until blended; set aside.

2 Sprinkle the gelatin over the evaporated milk in a medium saucepan. Let stand until softened, about 5 minutes. Heat over medium heat, stirring occasionally, until the gelatin is completely dissolved, about 2 minutes. Stir in the pumpkin mixture and cook, stirring constantly, until the mixture just begins to boil. Pour into a medium bowl; refrigerate until the filling begins to set, about 40 minutes.

3 Whisk the pumpkin mixture until smooth and creamy. With a rubber spatula, gently fold in the whipped topping until blended. Spoon into the crust, spreading it evenly; sprinkle with the pecans. Refrigerate until firm, at least 2 hours or up to overnight.

PER SERVING (⅛ of pie): 261 Cal, 5 g Fat, 1 g Sat Fat, 1 g Trans Fat, 28 mg Chol, 234 mg Sod, 48 g Carb, 2 g Fib, 7 g Prot, 150 mg Calc. **POINTS** value: **5.**

Food Note   Be sure to use pure canned pumpkin puree for this pie, not pumpkin pie mix, which contains sugar and spices.

Ricotta Cheese Tart with Candied Orange Peel

HANDS-ON PREP 30 MIN   **COOK** 1 HR 10 MIN   SERVES 8

10 reduced-fat vanilla wafer cookies,
      finely crushed
3   cups part-skim ricotta cheese
¾   cup confectioners' sugar
2   large eggs
1   egg white
1   tablespoon orange-flavored liqueur
      or 1 teaspoon orange extract
1   tablespoon grated lemon zest
      (about 2 lemons)
      Candied orange peel (optional)

1 Preheat the oven to 325°F. Spray a 9-inch springform pan with nonstick spray. Sprinkle the cookie crumbs evenly in the bottom of the pan.

2 Puree the ricotta with the confectioners' sugar in a food processor. Add the eggs, egg white, orange liqueur, and lemon zest; pulse just until blended.

3 Pour the cheese mixture on top of the crumbs in the pan; spread evenly. Bake until the center jiggles slightly, about 1 hour 10 minutes. Let cool in the pan on a rack about 1 hour. Refrigerate at least 4 hours or up to overnight.

4 Remove the tart from the pan. Sprinkle with candied orange peel (if using).

PER SERVING (⅛ of pie without candied orange peel): 222 Cal, 9 g Fat, 5 g Sat Fat, 0 g Trans Fat, 82 mg Chol, 156 mg Sod, 22 g Carb, 0 g Fib, 13 g Prot, 262 mg Calc. **POINTS** value: **5.**

How We Did It   Candied orange peel sprinkled along the rim of the pie is an easy, impressive, and tasty garnish. Here's how to make it: Remove the peel from 2 medium oranges; cut into ¼-inch-wide strips. Combine the orange peel, ½ cup water, and ¼ cup sugar in a small saucepan; bring to a boil. Reduce the heat and simmer until the peel is soft and translucent, about 10 minutes; drain well. Place 3 tablespoons sugar on a piece of wax paper. Toss the orange peel with the sugar until well coated. Spread the candied peel on a baking sheet; set aside until completely dry, about 1 hour.

RICOTTA CHEESE TART
WITH CANDIED ORANGE PEEL

Amaretti, Pear, and Cranberry Crumble

HANDS-ON PREP 20 MIN   COOK 35 MIN   SERVES 4

- ¼ cup sugar
- 1 tablespoon all-purpose flour
- 1 teaspoon cinnamon
- ¼ teaspoon salt
- 4 ripe medium pears (1½ pounds), halved, cored, and cut into 1-inch chunks
- ½ cup dried cranberries
- 1 tablespoon fresh lemon juice
- 8 amaretti cookies, coarsely crushed (½ cup)
- 1 tablespoon unsalted butter, melted

1 Preheat the oven to 450°F. Spray a 1½-quart baking dish with nonstick spray.

2 To make the filling, combine the sugar, flour, cinnamon, and salt in a large bowl. Add the pears, cranberries, and lemon juice; toss to mix well. Spoon into the baking dish. Sprinkle with the amaretti and drizzle with the melted butter. Bake until the pears are tender and the mixture is bubbly, about 35 minutes. Let cool on a rack about 20 minutes. Serve warm or at room temperature.

PER SERVING (¼ of crumble): 267 Cal, 4 g Fat, 2 g Sat Fat, 0 g Trans Fat, 8 mg Chol, 209 mg Sod, 61 g Carb, 7 g Fib, 1 g Prot, 28 mg Calc. *POINTS* value: *5.*

Food Note Amaretti are small dome-shaped Italian cookies that are simply bursting with almond flavor; they are often served as an after-dinner treat with coffee or dessert wine. Amaretti cookies can be found in the gourmet section of most supermarkets and in specialty food stores. If amaretti are not available, reduced-fat gingersnap cookies make a nice alternative.

Triple Berry-Maple Crisp

HANDS-ON PREP 20 MIN   COOK 35 MIN   SERVES 6

FILLING

2   cups blueberries (about 1 pint)
1   (6-ounce) container raspberries
1   (6-ounce) container blackberries
¼   cup sugar
2   tablespoons pure maple syrup
1   tablespoon grated lemon zest
    (about 2 lemons)
1   tablespoon cornstarch
¼   teaspoon salt

TOPPING

½   cup rolled (old-fashioned) oats
¼   cup whole-wheat pastry flour
¼   cup packed brown sugar
1   teaspoon cinnamon
1   tablespoon unsalted butter, melted
1   tablespoon canola oil
Pinch salt

1 Preheat the oven to 375°F. Spray a 1½-quart baking dish with nonstick spray.

2 To make the filling, combine the filling ingredients in a large bowl; spoon into the baking dish.

3 To make the topping, with a wooden spoon, stir together the topping ingredients in a medium bowl. Squeeze the mixture together to form a loose ball, then break it into small pieces and sprinkle evenly over the filling. Bake until the filling is thick and bubbly and the topping is golden, about 35 minutes, loosely covering the crisp with foil during the last 15 minutes to prevent overbrowning, if necessary.

PER SERVING (⅙ of crisp): 213 Cal, 5 g Fat, 1 g Sat Fat, 0 g Trans Fat, 5 mg Chol, 151 mg Sod, 42 g Carb, 5 g Fib, 3 g Prot, 41 mg Calc. **POINTS** value: **4.**

Good Idea   If fresh berries aren't available, use a 12-ounce package of frozen mixed berries; no need to thaw them.

GINGER BISCUIT–TOPPED
PEACH-BLACKBERRY COBBLER

Ginger Biscuit–Topped Peach–Blackberry Cobbler

HANDS-ON PREP 15 MIN   COOK 30 MIN   SERVES 6

FILLING

5   ripe medium peaches, halved, pitted, and
    cut into 1-inch chunks
1   (6-ounce) container blackberries
½   cup sugar
1   teaspoon almond extract
½   teaspoon cinnamon
Pinch salt

TOPPING

1¼ cups reduced-fat baking mix
6   tablespoons fat-free milk
2   tablespoons unsalted butter, melted
2   tablespoons sugar
1   tablespoon finely chopped crystallized ginger

1 Preheat the oven to 400°F. Spray six 8-ounce custard cups or ramekins with nonstick spray.

2 To make the filling, toss together the filling ingredients in a medium bowl. Spoon into the custard cups, dividing evenly.

3 To make the topping, combine the topping ingredients in a medium bowl. Spoon evenly in dollops over the filling. Place the cups on a baking sheet for easy handling. Bake until the topping is golden and the filling is bubbly, about 30 minutes. Serve warm or at room temperature.

PER SERVING (1 cobbler): 264 Cal, 6 g Fat, 3 g Sat Fat, 0 g Trans Fat, 10 mg Chol, 325 mg Sod, 51 g Carb, 3 g Fib, 4 g Prot, 130 mg Calc. **POINTS** value: **5.**

Express Lane   In most recipes, frozen peaches can easily be substituted for fresh peaches. Look for those that are unsweetened.

Blueberry Buckle

HANDS-ON PREP 20 MIN   COOK 45 MIN   SERVES 8

FILLING

1 cup all-purpose flour

1 teaspoon baking powder

½ teaspoon ground cardamom

¼ teaspoon salt

½ cup low-fat buttermilk

½ cup sugar

1 large egg

2 tablespoons canola oil

2 tablespoons unsalted butter, melted

2 cups blueberries (about 1 pint)

TOPPING

3 tablespoons all-purpose flour

2 tablespoons sugar

1 tablespoon canola oil

½ teaspoon cinnamon

1 Preheat the oven to 375°F. Spray a 1½-quart baking dish with nonstick spray.

2 To make the filling, whisk together the flour, baking powder, cardamom, and salt in a large bowl. Whisk together the buttermilk, sugar, egg, oil, and butter in a small bowl until blended. Add the buttermilk mixture to the flour mixture, stirring just until moistened. With a rubber spatula, gently fold in the blueberries. Spoon into the baking dish.

3 To make the topping, stir together the topping ingredients in a small bowl; sprinkle evenly over the filling. Bake until browned and bubbly, about 45 minutes. Let cool on a rack about 20 minutes. Serve warm or at room temperature.

PER SERVING (⅛ of buckle): 236 Cal, 9 g Fat, 3 g Sat Fat, 0 g Trans Fat, 35 mg Chol, 160 mg Sod, 36 g Carb, 2 g Fib, 4 g Prot, 63 mg Calc. **POINTS** value: **5.**

Food Note   A time-honored recipe, a buckle is a single-layer cake with fruit or berries either sprinkled on top of, or folded into, a thick batter which is then sprinkled with a crumb topping. It is called a buckle, as the topping seems to buckle up as it bakes. Blueberries are the most commonly used fruit, but just about any berry or fruit you like will work.

Tropical Fruit and Yogurt Pavlova

HANDS-ON PREP 25 MIN   COOK 3 HR   SERVES 8

MERINGUE

4   egg whites, at room temperature
¼   teaspoon cream of tartar
¾   cup sugar
¾   teaspoon vanilla extract
⅔   cup + 2 tablespoons flaked sweetened
    coconut, toasted

FILLING

2   cups (½-inch) diced fresh pineapple
1   ripe papaya, peeled, halved, seeded, and cut
    into ½-inch dice (about 2 cups)

1   ripe mango, peeled, pitted, and cut into
    ½-inch dice (about 1 cup)
2   kiwi fruit, peeled and cut into ½-inch dice
    (about 1 cup)
3   tablespoons sugar
1   teaspoon coconut extract
1   cup plain reduced-fat (2%) Greek-style yogurt

1 Preheat the oven to 200°F. Line a large baking sheet with foil. Use a plate and a toothpick to lightly trace a 9-inch circle onto the foil.

2 To make the meringue, with an electric mixer on medium speed, beat the egg whites and cream of tartar in a large bowl until soft peaks form. Increase the speed to medium-high. Sprinkle in the sugar, 2 tablespoons at a time, beating until stiff, glossy peaks form. Beat in the vanilla. Fold in ⅔ cup of the coconut. Using a narrow metal spatula, spread the meringue within the drawn circle to make a "nest" with a 1-inch-high edge. Bake until crisp and dry, about 3 hours. Turn the oven off; leave the meringue in the oven until crisp and dry, about 30 more minutes. Let cool on the baking sheet on a rack about 30 minutes. Gently lift the meringue off the foil and place on a serving plate.

3 Meanwhile, to make the filling, toss together all the filling ingredients except the yogurt in a large bowl. Let stand at room temperature until the fruit begins to release its juices, about 30 minutes.

4 To assemble, spread the yogurt over the bottom of the meringue. Spoon the fruit mixture on top and sprinkle with the remaining 2 tablespoons of coconut. Cut into 8 wedges and serve at once.

PER SERVING (⅛ of pavlova): 221 Cal, 3 g Fat, 3 g Sat Fat, 0 g Trans Fat, 2 mg Chol, 71 mg Sod, 45 g Carb, 3 g Fib, 4 g Prot, 82 mg Calc. *POINTS* value: *4.*

Chocolate-Cappuccino Éclairs

HANDS-ON PREP 40 MIN   COOK 1 HR   SERVES 8

PASTRY CREAM

¼ cup granulated sugar

1 large egg

1 teaspoon vanilla extract

3 tablespoons unsweetened cocoa powder

2 tablespoons cornstarch

1 teaspoon instant espresso powder

½ teaspoon cinnamon

⅔ cup fat-free milk

¼ cup thawed frozen fat-free whipped topping

CREAM PUFF DOUGH

1 cup water

3 tablespoons canola oil

1 tablespoon unsalted butter

1 teaspoon granulated sugar

¼ teaspoon salt

1 cup all-purpose flour

2 large eggs

1 egg white

1 tablespoon confectioners' sugar, for sprinkling

1 To make the pastry cream, whisk together the granulated sugar, egg, and vanilla in a bowl. Whisk in the cocoa, cornstarch, espresso powder, and cinnamon. Bring the milk to a boil in a small saucepan; whisk in the cocoa mixture. Return the milk mixture to the saucepan and bring to a boil. Cook, whisking, until thickened. Spoon into a bowl. Press a piece of plastic wrap onto the surface; refrigerate until cool. Fold in the whipped topping; refrigerate.

2 Preheat the oven to 400°F. Lightly spray a large baking sheet with nonstick spray; line with parchment paper.

3 To make the cream puff dough, combine the water, oil, butter, granulated sugar, and salt in a medium saucepan and set over medium-high heat. Cook until the butter melts and the mixture boils, about 3 minutes. Stir in the flour all at once; cook, stirring constantly with a wooden spoon, until the dough begins to pull away from the side of the pan, 1–2 minutes. Remove the saucepan from the heat and stir in the eggs and egg white, one at a time, beating vigorously after each addition until the dough is smooth and shiny.

4 Fill a large pastry bag (no need to use a tip) with the dough. Pipe onto the baking sheet to form eight 4-inch-long x 2-inch-wide fingers. Bake until golden, about 35 minutes. Turn off the oven. Make a small slit in one end of each éclair. Return to the oven for 10 minutes. Let cool completely on a rack.

5 To assemble the éclairs, with a small knife, make a hole in one end of each éclair. Spoon the pastry cream into a pastry bag fitted with a ¼-inch plain tip. Pipe about 2 tablespoons pastry cream into each éclair. Dust with the confectioners' sugar. Serve within 2 hours.

PER SERVING (1 éclair): 193 Cal, 9 g Fat, 2 g Sat Fat, 0 g Trans Fat, 83 mg Chol, 106 mg Sod, 24 g Carb, 1 g Fib, 5 g Prot, 18 mg Calc. **POINTS** value: **4.**

CHOCOLATE-CAPPUCCINO
ÉCLAIRS

Cherry Strudel

HANDS-ON PREP 20 MIN   COOK 25 MIN   SERVES 10

3   **cups pitted tart fresh cherries**
    (from about 1½ pounds)
1   **cup granulated sugar**
3   **tablespoons cornstarch**
1   **tablespoon fresh lemon juice**
½   **teaspoon cinnamon**
¼   **cup plain dried bread crumbs**
¼   **cup sliced or slivered almonds, finely ground**
12 **(12 x 17-inch) sheets frozen phyllo dough,**
    thawed
1   **tablespoon confectioners' sugar**

1 To make the filling, combine the cherries, ¾ cup of the sugar, the cornstarch, lemon juice, and cinnamon in a medium saucepan and set over medium-high heat; bring to a boil. Reduce the heat to medium. Cook, stirring constantly until thickened and bubbly, about 2 minutes. Remove the saucepan from the heat; set aside until cool, about 30 minutes.

2 Preheat the oven to 400°F.

3 Combine the bread crumbs, almonds, and the remaining ¼ cup of sugar in a small bowl. Lay 1 phyllo sheet on a work surface with a long side facing you. Keep the remaining phyllo covered with a damp towel and plastic wrap to prevent it from drying out. Lightly spray the phyllo with nonstick spray; sprinkle with about 1 tablespoon of the crumb mixture. Continue layering with the remaining phyllo and crumb mixture, lightly spraying each sheet of phyllo with nonstick spray to make 12 layers in all.

4 Spoon the cherry filling over the phyllo, leaving a 2-inch border. Fold the short sides of phyllo over the filling, then roll up jelly-roll style. Do not roll too tightly or the phyllo might tear.

5 Place the strudel on a diagonal, seam side down, on a large baking sheet. Lightly spray the strudel with nonstick spray. Cut four 1-inch slits in the top of the strudel to allow the steam to escape. Bake until the filling is hot and the phyllo is golden brown, about 20 minutes. Let cool completely on the baking sheet on a rack at least 45 minutes. Just before serving, dust with the confectioners' sugar.

PER SERVING (1/10 of strudel): 229 Cal, 2 g Fat, 0 g Sat Fat, 0 g Trans Fat, 00 mg Chol, 121 mg Sod, 51 g Carb, 2 g Fib, 4 g Prot, 22 mg Calc. ***POINTS*** value: **4.**

Faux Crêpes Suzette

HANDS-ON PREP 10 MIN   COOK 3 MIN   SERVES 4

½ cup fresh orange juice

3 tablespoons unsalted butter, cut into 3 pieces

3 tablespoons packed light brown sugar

1 teaspoon cornstarch

⅛ teaspoon salt

2 tablespoons orange-flavored liqueur

1 tablespoon grated orange zest

8 (9-inch) ready-to-use crêpes (part of a
    5-ounce package)

Confectioners' sugar

1 Combine the orange juice, butter, brown sugar, cornstarch, and salt in a medium nonstick skillet and set over medium-high heat. Cook, stirring constantly, until the butter is melted and the mixture bubbles and thickens, about 2 minutes. Reduce the heat to medium. Add the liqueur and orange zest to the skillet and bring to a boil; boil 30 seconds.

2 Fold each crêpe in quarters and arrange on a platter. Spoon the sauce over and dust with confectioners' sugar. Serve at once.

PER SERVING (2 crêpes and 3 tablespoons sauce): 254 Cal, 10 g Fat, 6 g Sat Fat, 1 g , Trans Fat, 32 mg Chol, 179 mg Sod, 36 g Carb, 1 g Fib, 2 g Prot, 35 mg Calc. *POINTS* value: *6.*

Food Note   As the story goes, crêpes Suzette was created out of a mistake. Henri Carpentier, a 14-year-old assistant waiter in a Parisian café, was preparing dessert for the future King Edward VII of England and his companion, Suzette. Henri was working in front of a chafing dish and the cordial mixture accidentally caught fire. He tasted the sauce and found the flavor so delectable that he served the dessert anyway.

Brownies Squares & Cookies

Chapter 3

Fudgy Cocoa Brownies

HANDS-ON PREP 15 MIN   COOK 20 MIN   MAKES 16

- ¾ **cup all-purpose flour**
- ½ **teaspoon baking powder**
- ¼ **teaspoon salt**
- 3 **tablespoons unsalted butter**
- ½ **cup unsweetened cocoa powder**
- 2 **teaspoons vanilla extract**
- ¾ **cup granulated sugar**
- ¼ **cup packed light brown sugar**
- 1 **large egg**
- 2 **egg whites**
- ¾ **cup walnuts, coarsely chopped**

1 Preheat the oven to 350°F. Line an 8-inch square baking pan with foil, allowing the foil to extend over the rim of the pan by 2 inches. Spray with nonstick spray.

2 Whisk together the flour, baking powder, and salt in a small bowl; set aside. Melt the butter in a medium saucepan set over low heat. Remove the saucepan from the heat. Whisk in the cocoa and vanilla; let stand 5 minutes. Add the granulated sugar, brown sugar, egg, and egg whites to the cocoa mixture; whisk until blended. Stir in the flour mixture until blended. Stir in the walnuts.

3 Scrape the batter into the baking pan and spread evenly. Bake until a toothpick inserted into the center comes out with moist crumbs clinging, 20–25 minutes. Let cool completely in the pan on a rack. Lift from the pan using the foil as handles; cut into 16 squares.

PER SERVING: (1 square): 140 Cal, 7 g Fat, 2 g Sat Fat, 0 g Trans Fat, 19 mg Chol, 65 mg Sod, 19 g Carb, 1 g Fib, 3 g Prot, 18 mg Calc. **POINTS** value: **3.**

Good Idea   For easier cutting, refrigerate the cooled brownies about 1 hour.

FUDGY COCOA BROWNIES

Toffee-Apple Blondies

HANDS-ON PREP 25 MIN   COOK 20 MIN   MAKES 16

3 tablespoons unsalted butter

½ cup all-purpose flour

½ cup whole-wheat flour

½ teaspoon baking powder

¼ teaspoon salt

½ cup packed dark brown sugar

2 egg whites

2 tablespoons dark corn syrup

1 teaspoon vanilla extract

1 small Granny Smith apple, peeled, cored, and cut into ½-inch pieces (about 1 cup)

4 tablespoons toffee bits

2 tablespoons finely chopped pecans

1 Melt the butter in a medium saucepan set over low heat. Continue to cook, swirling the pan occasionally, until the butter turns nut brown. Pour into a large bowl and let cool slightly.

2 Preheat the oven to 350°F. Line an 8-inch square baking pan with foil, allowing the foil to extend over the rim of the pan by 2 inches. Spray with nonstick spray.

3 Whisk together the all-purpose flour, whole-wheat flour, baking powder, and salt in a small bowl; set aside. Stir the brown sugar into the melted butter until combined. Add the egg whites, corn syrup, and vanilla; stir until well blended. Stir in the flour mixture. Stir in the apple and 3 tablespoons of the toffee bits.

4 Scrape the batter into the baking pan and spread evenly. Sprinkle with the remaining 1 tablespoon of toffee bits and the pecans. Bake until a toothpick inserted into the center comes out clean, 20–25 minutes. Let cool completely in the pan on a rack. Cover the pan and refrigerate about 1 hour for easier cutting. Lift from the pan using the foil as handles; cut into 16 squares.

PER SERVING (1 square): 101 Cal, 3 g Fat, 2 g Sat Fat, 0 g Trans Fat, 6 mg Chol, 65 mg Sod, 17 g Carb, 1 g Fib, 2 g Prot, 22 mg Calc. *POINTS* value: *2.*

Good Idea   These moist and cakey blondies are best stored in an airtight container in the refrigerator. They will keep up to 3 days. Look for packages of toffee bits in the candy aisle of the supermarket.

Maple-Glazed Raisin Bars

HANDS ON PREP 10 MIN   COOK TIME 20 MIN   MAKES 24

- 1   cup all-purpose flour
- ½   cup whole-wheat flour
- 2   teaspoons pumpkin pie spice
- 1   teaspoon baking soda
- ¼   teaspoon salt
- 1¼ cups unsweetened applesauce
- ¾   cup packed light brown sugar
- 2   tablespoons canola oil
- 1   cup dark raisins
- 2   tablespoons confectioners' sugar
- 2   tablespoons pure maple syrup

1 Preheat the oven to 350°F. Line a 9 x 13-inch baking pan with foil, allowing the foil extend over the rim of the pan by 2 inches. Spray with nonstick spray.

2 Whisk together the all-purpose flour, whole-wheat flour, pumpkin pie spice, baking soda, and salt in a medium bowl; set aside. With a wooden spoon, combine the applesauce, brown sugar, and oil in a large bowl until well blended. Add the flour mixture to the applesauce mixture and stir just until blended; stir in the raisins.

3 Scrape the batter into the pan and spread evenly. Bake until a toothpick inserted into the center comes out clean, 20–25 minutes. Place the pan on a rack.

4 Stir together the confectioners' sugar and maple syrup in a small bowl until smooth. Using a pastry brush, brush over the layer; let cool completely. Lift from the pan using the foil as handles; cut into 24 bars.

PER SERVING (1 bar): 94 Cal, 1 g Fat, 0 g Sat Fat, 0 g Trans Fat, 0 mg Chol, 81 mg Sod, 21 g Carb, 1 g Fib, 1 g Prot, 13 mg Calc. *POINTS* value: *2.*

Try It   If you're a fan of ginger, stir in ¼ cup chopped crystallized ginger with the raisins. If you don't have pumpkin pie spice, you can make your own: combine 1¼ teaspoons cinnamon, ½ teaspoon ground ginger, ⅛ teaspoon nutmeg, and ⅛ teaspoon ground allspice.

Easy Cherry-Berry Jam Squares

HANDS-ON PREP 20 MIN   COOK 25 MIN   MAKES 16

1   cup whole-wheat pastry flour
¾   cup quick-cooking (not instant) oats
½   cup packed light brown sugar
¼   cup pecans, finely chopped
½   teaspoon cinnamon
½   teaspoon baking soda
¼   teaspoon salt
1   egg white
2   tablespoons canola oil

1   tablespoon fat-free milk
1   (10-ounce) jar raspberry fruit spread
½   cup dried tart cherries, chopped

1 Preheat the oven to 350°F. Line a 9-inch square baking pan with foil, allowing the foil to extend over the rim of the pan by 2 inches. Spray with nonstick spray.

2 Combine the pastry flour, oats, brown sugar, pecans, cinnamon, baking soda, and salt in a large bowl. With a fork, beat together the egg white, oil, and milk in a small bowl. Add the egg mixture to the flour mixture, stirring until well blended. With your fingers, blend the mixture until moist crumbs form. Reserve ⅔ cup. Transfer the remaining oat mixture to the baking pan, pressing firmly to form an even layer. Bake until set and lightly browned along the edges, about 10 minutes.

3 Stir together the fruit spread and cherries in a small bowl; spread evenly over the hot crust. Crumble the reserved oat mixture on top. Bake until the jam is bubbly at the edges and the top is nicely browned, 15–20 minutes. Let cool completely in the pan on a rack. Lift from the pan using the foil as handles; cut into 16 squares.

PER SERVING (1 square): 149 Cal, 3 g Fat, 0 g Sat Fat, 0 g Trans Fat, 0 mg Chol, 85 mg Sod, 29 g Carb, 3 g Fib, 3 g Prot, 23 mg Calc. **POINTS** value: **3.**

How We Did It   Here's the easiest and neatest way to line a baking pan with foil: Turn the pan upside down. Press a piece of foil, shiny side facing out, over the pan to set the shape; lift up the foil. Turn the pan right side up. Lower the foil "pan" into the baking pan, smoothing it to create a tight fit.

Chocolate-Peanut Butter Squares

HANDS-ON PREP 15 MIN   COOK 5 MIN   MAKES 24

3   cups popped plain popcorn
2   cups crisp rice cereal
2   cups circle oat cereal
⅓   cup unsalted peanuts, chopped
1   tablespoon unsalted butter
1   ounce unsweetened chocolate, chopped
1   (7½-ounce) jar marshmallow crème
¼   cup creamy or chunky natural peanut butter
3   tablespoons unsweetened cocoa powder
1½ teaspoons vanilla extract

1 Line a 9 x 13-inch baking pan with foil, allowing the foil to extend over the rim of the pan by 2 inches. Spray with nonstick spray.

2 Combine the popcorn, rice cereal, oat cereal, and peanuts in a very large bowl.

3 Put the butter and chocolate in a large nonstick skillet and set over low heat. Cook, stirring, until melted, 1–2 minutes. Remove the skillet from the heat; add the marshmallow crème, peanut butter, cocoa powder, and vanilla. Return the skillet to the heat and cook, stirring, until well blended and hot, 2–3 minutes.

4 Scrape the marshmallow mixture on top of the cereal mixture. With a rubber spatula, stir vigorously until the cereal mixture is evenly coated. Scrape into the baking pan. Spray your hands with nonstick spray; press down firmly on the mixture to form an even layer; let cool completely. Lift from the pan using the foil as handles. With a serrated knife lightly sprayed with nonstick spray, cut into 24 squares.

PER SERVING (1 square): 87 Cal, 4 g Fat, 1 g Sat Fat, 0 g Trans Fat, 1 mg Chol, 38 mg Sod, 12 g Carb, 1 g Fib, 2 g Prot, 15 mg Calc. **POINTS** value: **2.**

Food Note   Natural peanut butter, once found only in health food stores, is now available in grocery stores. It is made from ground peanuts, with or without added salt. This peanut butter has a natural layer of oil on top. To redistribute the oil through the peanut butter, turn the jar upside down and let it stand about a day, until the oil is no longer visible.

Fresh Lemon-Lime Squares

HANDS-ON PREP 20 MIN   COOK 45 MIN   MAKES 16

- 1   cup all-purpose flour
- ¼   cup cornmeal
- ⅛   teaspoon baking powder
- ⅛   teaspoon salt
- 2   large eggs
- 1   egg white
- 1   teaspoon water
- 2   tablespoons unsalted butter, softened
- 1   cup granulated sugar
- 2   teaspoons grated lemon zest

- ⅓   cup fresh lemon juice
- 2   teaspoons grated lime zest
- 3   tablespoons fresh lime juice
- 1   tablespoon confectioners' sugar

1 Preheat the oven to 350°F. Line an 8-inch square baking pan with foil, allowing the foil to extend over the rim of the pan by 2 inches. Spray with nonstick spray.

2 Whisk together ⅔ cup of the flour, the cornmeal, baking powder, and salt in a small bowl; set aside. With a fork, beat together the eggs and egg white in a small bowl. Transfer 1 tablespoon of the beaten egg mixture to a cup; stir in the water. Set aside both egg mixtures.

3 With an electric mixer on low speed, beat the butter in a medium bowl until creamy. Add ¼ cup of the granulated sugar and beat until blended. Beat in the egg-water mixture. Add the flour mixture and beat until blended. Press the dough evenly onto the bottom and ¼ inch up the sides of the pan. Bake until golden brown, about 22 minutes.

4 Meanwhile, whisk together the remaining ⅓ cup of flour and ¾ cup of granulated sugar in a medium bowl. Whisk in the remaining egg mixture until blended. Add the lemon zest and juice and lime zest and juice, whisking until well blended.

5 Reduce the oven temperature to 300°F. Pour the lemon-lime mixture over the hot crust. Bake until the filling is set, 20–25 minutes. Let cool in the pan on a rack. Refrigerate until cold, at least 1 hour or up to 8 hours. Dust with the confectioners' sugar. Lift from the pan using the foil as handles; cut into 16 squares.

PER SERVING (1 square): 112 Cal, 2 g Fat, 1 g Sat Fat, 0 g Trans Fat, 30 mg Chol, 35 mg Sod, 21 g Carb, 0 g Fib, 2 g Prot, 9 mg Calc. **POINTS** value: **2.**

How We Did It   You will need about 3 lemons and 2 limes to get the amount of juice needed here.

Chewy Chocolate-Walnut Cookies

HANDS-ON PREP 15 MIN   COOK 12 MIN   MAKES 24

2⅓ cups confectioners' sugar
¾ cup Dutch-process cocoa powder
⅛ teaspoon salt
3 egg whites, at room temperature
2 teaspoons vanilla extract
1 cup walnuts, chopped

1 Place the oven racks in the upper and lower thirds of the oven and preheat the oven to 350°F. Line 2 large baking sheets with parchment paper.

2 Sift together the confectioners' sugar, cocoa, and salt into a medium bowl. With an electric mixer on low speed, beat the egg whites into the cocoa mixture until blended. Increase the speed to high. Beat about 1 minute. Beat in the vanilla, then stir in the walnuts.

3 Drop the dough by level tablespoonfuls onto the baking sheets about 2 inches apart, making a total of 24 cookies. Bake until shiny, cracked, and firm to the touch, 12–15 minutes. Let cool completely on the baking sheets on racks.

PER SERVING (1 cookie): 82 Cal, 3 g Fat, 0 g Sat Fat, 0 g Trans Fat, 0 mg Chol, 20 mg Sod, 14 g Carb, 1 g Fib, 2 g Prot, 8 mg Calc. **POINTS** value: **2.**

Food Note   There are two kinds of unsweetened cocoa powder: natural and Dutch process. Natural cocoa has full, rich chocolate flavor and is the type used most often in baking. Dutch-process cocoa has been treated with an alkali, which mellows its flavor and gives baked goods a very deep color.

DOUBLE ALMOND
MACAROONS, PAGE 76, AND
WHITE AND DARK
CHOCOLATE CHUNK COOKIES

White and Dark Chocolate Chunk Cookies

HANDS-ON PREP 15 MIN   COOK 9 MIN   MAKES 24

½ cup quick-cooking (not instant) oats
1 cup all-purpose flour
½ teaspoon baking soda
¼ teaspoon salt
4 tablespoons unsalted butter, melted and cooled
¾ cup packed light brown sugar
1 large egg
1 teaspoon vanilla extract

2 ounces white chocolate, cut into ¼-inch pieces
2 ounces bittersweet or semisweet chocolate, cut into ¼-inch pieces

1 Place the oven racks in the upper and lower thirds of the oven and preheat the oven to 350°F. Spray 2 large baking sheets with nonstick spray.

2 Put the oats in a blender and process until finely ground. Combine the oats, flour, baking soda, and salt in a small bowl; set aside. With an electric mixer on low speed, beat the butter, brown sugar, egg, and vanilla in a large bowl until well blended. Add the flour mixture and beat until blended. Combine 1 tablespoon each of the white and bittersweet chocolates in a small bowl; set aside. Stir the remaining white and bittersweet chocolates into the dough.

3 Drop the dough by level tablespoonfuls onto the baking sheets 2 inches apart, making a total of 24 cookies. With a glass dipped in flour or with your fingers, press each mound to make 2-inch rounds. Sprinkle the cookies evenly with the reserved chocolate, pressing lightly so it adheres. Bake until lightly browned along the edges, 9–11 minutes, rotating the baking sheets halfway through the baking. Let cool on the baking sheets on racks about 1 minute. With a spatula, transfer the cookies to racks and let cool completely.

PER SERVING (1 cookie): 96 Cal, 4 g Fat, 2 g Sat Fat, 0 g Trans Fat, 14 mg Chol, 59 mg Sod, 15 g Carb, 1 g Fib, 1 g Prot, 15 mg Calc. **POINTS** value: **2.**

Express Lane Substitute ⅓ cup each semisweet chocolate chips and white chocolate chips for the chopped chocolate, and you'll save time in the kitchen.

Oatmeal-Cranberry Classics

HANDS-ON PREP 20 MIN   COOK 12 MIN   MAKES 30

1   cup whole-wheat pastry flour
½   teaspoon baking soda
½   teaspoon cinnamon
¼   teaspoon salt
½   cup packed light brown sugar
¼   cup granulated sugar
2   tablespoons unsalted butter, softened
2   tablespoons canola oil
1   egg white

1½ teaspoons vanilla extract
¼   cup unsweetened applesauce
1½ cups quick-cooking (not instant) oats
½   cup dried cranberries

1 Place the oven racks in the upper and lower thirds of the oven and preheat the oven to 350°F. Spray 2 large baking sheets with nonstick spray.

2 Whisk together the pastry flour, baking soda, cinnamon, and salt in a small bowl; set aside. With an electric mixer on low speed, beat the brown sugar, granulated sugar, butter, oil, egg white, and vanilla in a large bowl until well blended, about 1 minute. Beat in the applesauce. Add the flour mixture and beat just until blended. Stir in the oats and cranberries.

3 Drop the dough by level tablespoonfuls onto the baking sheets about 2½ inches apart, making a total of 30 cookies. With the back of a spoon, spread the mounds to make 2-inch cookies. Bake until the edges are lightly browned, about 12 minutes. Let cool on the baking sheets on racks about 2 minutes. With a spatula, transfer the cookies to racks and let cool completely.

PER SERVING (1 cookie): 73 Cal, 2 g Fat, 1 g Sat Fat, 0 g Trans Fat, 2 mg Chol, 45 mg Sod, 13 g Carb, 1 g Fib, 1 g Prot, 8 mg Calc. *POINTS* value: *1.*

Try It   Chunky, chewy oatmeal cookies are a cookie-jar classic. Ours have just the right touch of cinnamon and vanilla, along with a generous amount of good-for-you oatmeal and antioxidant-rich dried cranberries. If you like, substitute dried cherries, blueberries, or chopped dried apricots for the cranberries.

Brown Sugar and Spice Drop Cookies

HANDS-ON PREP 20 MIN   COOK 8 MIN   MAKES 36

- 4 tablespoons unsalted butter
- 1½ cups all-purpose flour
- 1 teaspoon cinnamon
- ½ teaspoon ground ginger
- ½ teaspoon baking soda
- ½ teaspoon salt
- ¾ cup packed dark brown sugar
- ¼ cup honey

- 1 egg white
- 2 teaspoons vanilla extract
- ⅓ cup fat-free sour cream
- 36 pecan halves

1 Place the oven racks in the upper and lower thirds of the oven and preheat the oven to 350°F. Spray 2 large baking sheets with nonstick spray.

2 Melt the butter in a small saucepan over low heat. Continue to cook, swirling the pan occasionally, until the butter turns nut brown, about 2 minutes. Pour the butter into a small bowl and let cool to room temperature.

3 Whisk together the flour, cinnamon, ginger, baking soda, and salt in a small bowl; set aside. Stir together the brown sugar, honey, egg white, and vanilla in a large bowl until blended. Stir in the browned butter, then the sour cream. Add the flour mixture and stir until blended.

4 Drop the dough by teaspoonfuls onto the baking sheets about 2 inches apart, making a total of 36 cookies. Lightly press a pecan half into each cookie. Bake until the cookies spring back when lightly pressed, 8–10 minutes, rotating the baking sheets halfway through the baking. Let cool on the baking sheets on racks about 2 minutes. With a spatula, transfer the cookies to racks and let cool completely.

PER SERVING (1 cookie): 68 Cal, 2 g Fat, 1 g Sat Fat, 0 g Trans Fat, 4 mg Chol, 57 mg Sod, 11 g Carb, 0 g Fib, 1 g Prot, 10 mg Calc. **POINTS** value: **2.**

How We Did It Browning the butter adds rich nutty flavor to these tempting cookies. When browning butter, watch it carefully, as the flecks of milk solids in the butter can go from browned to burnt very quickly. Be sure to include all the flavorful brown flecks when adding the butter to the dough.

Double Almond Macaroons

HANDS-ON PREP 15 MIN   COOK 15 MIN   MAKES 16

1   cup slivered almonds
⅔   cup sugar
⅛   teaspoon salt
1   egg white
½   teaspoon vanilla extract
¼   teaspoon almond extract
3   tablespoons sliced almonds, coarsely chopped

1 Place an oven rack in the upper third of the oven and preheat the oven to 350°F. Line a large baking sheet with parchment paper.

2 Put the slivered almonds, sugar, and salt in a food processor; process until the almonds are very finely ground, about 1 minute. Add the egg white, vanilla, and almond extract; pulse 10 times, or until the dough comes together; scrape into a small bowl.

3 Drop the dough by scant tablespoonfuls onto the baking sheet about 2½ inches apart, making a total of 16 cookies. Lightly brush the cookies with water and flatten them slightly; sprinkle evenly with the sliced almonds. Bake until golden brown, about 15 minutes. Slide the parchment paper onto a rack and let cool completely. Peel the macaroons off the parchment paper.

PER SERVING (1 macaroon): 79 Cal, 4 g Fat, 0 g Sat Fat, 0 g Trans Fat, 0 mg Chol, 21 mg Sod, 10 g Carb, 1 g Fib, 2 g Prot, 20 mg Calc. *POINTS* value: *2.*

Good Idea   The combination of chocolate and almond is classic and delicious. If you like, dip half of each macaroon in melted semisweet or bittersweet chocolate, then place on a piece of wax paper until set. When storing the chocolate-coated cookies, be sure to separate the layers with sheets of wax paper.

Almond-Citrus Tuiles

HANDS-ON PREP 30 MIN   COOK 6 MIN   MAKES 18

- ¾ **cup sliced almonds**
- ⅓ **cup confectioners' sugar**
- 3 **tablespoons superfine sugar**
- 1 **large egg, at room temperature**
- ½ **teaspoon vanilla extract**
- 1½ **teaspoons grated lime zest**
- 1 **tablespoon all-purpose flour**

1 Place the oven racks in the upper and lower thirds of the oven and preheat the oven to 375°F. Generously spray 2 large baking sheets with nonstick spray.

2 Put ⅓ cup of the almonds and the confectioners' sugar in a food processor; process until the almonds are very finely ground. Stir together the superfine sugar, egg, and vanilla in a small bowl until well blended. Stir in the almond mixture, the remaining almonds, and the lime zest. Sprinkle with the flour and stir to combine.

3 Drop 5 mounds of the batter on each baking sheet, using 2 level teaspoonfuls for each mound, spacing them about 4 inches apart. Using a fork dipped in cold water, spread each mound to make a 2¼-inch round, being sure to evenly distribute the almonds. Bake until the edges are browned but the centers are still pale, 6–7 minutes.

4 Push a metal pancake spatula under a cookie to lift it, then drape the cookie over a rolling pin, gently pressing so it curves. Repeat with the remaining cookies. If the cookies harden before you can shape them, return the cookies to the oven for about 30 seconds. Cool, wash, dry, and spray the baking sheets before making the remaining 8 cookies.

PER SERVING (1 cookie): 45 Cal, 2 g Fat, 0 g Sat Fat, 0 g Trans Fat, 12 mg Chol, 4 mg Sod, 5 g Carb, 0 g Fib, 1 g Prot, 11 mg Calc. **POINTS** value: **1.**

How We Did It   To make superfine sugar at home, process regular sugar in a food processor until very finely ground, which will take about 1 minute.

Old-Fashioned Ginger Cookies

HANDS-ON PREP 30 MIN   COOK 10 MINUTES   MAKES 36

2   cups whole-wheat pastry flour
1   teaspoon baking soda
1   teaspoon cinnamon
1   teaspoon ground ginger
¼   cup canola oil
¼   cup dark molasses
1   large egg
2   teaspoons grated peeled fresh ginger
1   cup + 3 tablespoons sugar

1 Place the oven racks in the upper and lower thirds of the oven and preheat the oven to 350°F. Line 2 large baking sheets with parchment paper.

2 Whisk together the pastry flour, baking soda, cinnamon, and ground ginger in a medium bowl. Whisk together the oil, molasses, egg, and fresh ginger in a large bowl until smooth; whisk in 1 cup of the sugar. Add the flour mixture and stir until blended. Let the dough rest about 10 minutes.

3 Spread the remaining 3 tablespoons of sugar on a small plate. Roll scant tablespoonfuls of the dough into 1-inch balls, making a total of 36 balls. Dip the tops of the balls in the sugar and place, sugar side up, on the baking sheets about 2 inches apart. Bake until the cookies are cracked, soft in the center, and firm along the edges, 10–12 minutes. Let cool on the baking sheets on racks about 2 minutes. With a spatula, transfer the cookies to racks and let cool completely.

PER SERVING (1 cookie): 71 Cal, 2 g Fat, 0 g Sat Fat, 0 g Trans Fat, 6 mg Chol, 38 mg Sod, 13 g Carb, 1 g Fib, 1 g Prot, 9 mg Calc. **POINTS** value: **1.**

Food Note   For these cookies, you can use either light or dark molasses but not blackstrap. Light molasses comes from the first boiling of the sugar syrup and has a mild flavor and is light colored. Dark molasses comes from the second boiling and is thicker, darker, and not as sweet. It is usually used for gingerbread, ginger cookies, and Indian pudding. Blackstrap molasses comes from the third boiling and is what is left in the barrel; it is very dark, very thick, and somewhat bitter.

Peanut Butter Cookies

HANDS-ON PREP 25 MIN   COOK 8 MIN   MAKES 36

1   cup all-purpose flour
¼   cup whole-wheat flour
½   teaspoon baking soda
¼   teaspoon salt
¾   cup packed dark brown sugar
¼   cup chunky peanut butter
3   tablespoons unsalted butter, melted
    and cooled

1   large egg
1   teaspoon vanilla extract
1   (3.5-ounce) box chocolate-covered peanuts
⅓   cup peanut butter chips, chopped

1 Place the oven racks in the upper and lower thirds of the oven and preheat the oven to 350°F. Line 2 large baking sheets with parchment paper.

2 Combine the all-purpose flour, whole-wheat flour, baking soda, and salt in a small bowl; set aside. With an electric mixer on low speed, beat the brown sugar, peanut butter, and butter in a large bowl until combined. Add the egg and vanilla and beat until well blended. Add the flour mixture and beat until blended. Stir in the chocolate-covered peanuts and peanut butter chips.

3 Roll scant tablespoonfuls of the dough into 1-inch balls, making a total of 36 cookies. If necessary, dust your hands with flour to prevent the dough from sticking. Place the balls on the baking sheets about 2 inches apart, then press with a glass dipped in flour to make 1½-inch rounds. Bake until set, 8–10 minutes, rotating the baking sheets halfway through the baking. Let cool on the baking sheets on racks about 1 minute. With a spatula, transfer the cookies to racks and let cool completely.

PER SERVING (1 cookie): 77 Cal, 3 g Fat, 2 g Sat Fat, 0 g Trans Fat, 9 mg Chol, 48 mg Sod, 11 g Carb, 0 g Fib, 2 g Prot, 10 mg Calc. **POINTS** Value: *2.*

How We Did It To give these cookies a crunchy edge and chewy center—the way we think they are at their most delicious—be sure not to overbake them.

FRESH LEMON-LIME
SQUARES, PAGE 70,
APRICOT RUGELACH,
OATMEAL-CRANBERRY
CLASSICS, PAGE 74, AND
CHOCOLATE-ORANGE
SPIRALS, PAGE 82

Apricot Rugelach

HANDS-ON PREP 35 MIN   COOK 22 MIN   MAKES 32

DOUGH

1½ cups all-purpose flour

2   tablespoons sugar

½   teaspoon salt

⅓   cup low-fat cream cheese (Neufchâtel),
     cut into 4 pieces

3   tablespoons cold unsalted butter, cut
     into pieces

2   tablespoons canola oil

2   tablespoons cold water

FILLING

⅔   cup apricot fruit spread

⅔   cup dried fruit bits, chopped

3   tablespoons sugar

¼   teaspoon cinnamon

1 To make the dough, put the flour, sugar, and salt in a food processor; pulse until combined. Evenly distribute the cream cheese and butter on top of the flour mixture; pulse until the mixture resembles coarse meal. Drizzle with the oil and pulse just until blended. Drizzle with the water and pulse just until the dough begins to come together. Gather the dough into a ball and cut in half. Flatten each half into a disk. Roll each disk between pieces of plastic wrap to an 11-inch round. Refrigerate until cold and firm, at least 1 hour or up to overnight.

2 Place the oven racks in the upper and lower thirds of the oven and preheat the oven to 350°F. Line 2 large baking sheets with parchment paper.

3 Working with 1 dough round at a time (keep the remaining round refrigerated), peel off the top piece of plastic wrap, then place it back on the dough. Flip the dough over; peel off the top piece of plastic wrap and discard. Spread ⅓ cup of the apricot spread over the dough, leaving a ¾-inch border. Sprinkle evenly with ⅓ cup of the dried fruit. With your fingers, gently press the filling into the dough. Combine the sugar and cinnamon in a small bowl. Sprinkle 3½ teaspoons of the cinnamon sugar over the filling.

4 Using a pizza cutter or sharp knife, cut the dough round in quarters, then cut each quarter into 4 wedges. Beginning at the outer edge of each wedge, roll up to form a crescent. Discard the plastic wrap. Place the crescents, pointed end down, on the baking sheets about 2 inches apart. Sprinkle with 1 teaspoon of the cinnamon sugar. Repeat with the remaining dough, fruit spread, dried fruit, and cinnamon sugar, making a total of 32 rugelach in all. Bake just until golden brown along the edges, 22–25 minutes, rotating the baking sheets halfway through the baking. With a spatula, transfer the rugelach to racks and let cool completely.

PER SERVING (1 rugelach): 75 Cal, 3 g Fat, 1 g Sat Fat, 0 g Trans Fat, 5 mg Chol, 48 mg Sod, 12 g Carb, 1 g Fib, 1 g Prot, 7 mg Calc. **POINTS** value: **2.**

Chocolate-Orange Spirals

HANDS-ON PREP 30 MIN   COOK 8 MIN   MAKES 36

1   **cup all-purpose flour**
¼   **teaspoon baking soda**
⅛   **teaspoon salt**
4   **tablespoons unsalted butter, softened**
⅔   **cup sugar**
1   **egg white**
1   **teaspoon vanilla extract**
1   **teaspoon grated orange zest**
1   **teaspoon fresh orange juice**
2   **tablespoons unsweetened cocoa powder**
½   **ounce bittersweet chocolate, grated**

1 Stir together the flour, baking soda, and salt in a small bowl; set aside. With an electric mixer on low speed, beat the butter and sugar in a medium bowl until well blended. Add the egg white and vanilla; beat until smooth. Add the flour mixture and beat just until blended. Transfer half of the dough to a small bowl and stir in the orange zest. Stir the orange juice, cocoa powder, and grated chocolate into the remaining dough.

2 Pat the chocolate dough into a rectangle on a 12-inch-long piece of plastic wrap. Cover with another piece of plastic wrap. Roll out the dough to form a 5 x 8-inch rectangle. Repeat with the orange dough. Refrigerate the doughs about 5 minutes. Remove the top sheets of plastic wrap from the doughs. Flip the orange dough on top of the chocolate dough; remove the plastic wrap. Using the bottom sheet of plastic wrap to help you and beginning with a long side, roll up the dough, jelly-roll style, to form a tight log. Wrap in the plastic wrap and roll into a 9-inch-long log. Refrigerate until firm, at least 4 hours or up to 2 days.

3 Meanwhile, place the oven racks in the upper and lower thirds of the oven and preheat the oven to 350°F. Spray 2 large baking sheets with nonstick spray.

4 Cut the log into ¼-inch-thick slices, making a total of 36 slices. Place on the baking sheets about 1 inch apart. Bake until golden brown, 8–10 minutes, rotating the baking sheets halfway through the baking. With a spatula, transfer the cookies to racks and let cool completely.

PER SERVING (1 cookie): 42 Cal, 2 g Fat, 1 g Sat Fat, 0 g Trans Fat, 3 mg Chol, 19 mg Sod, 7 g Carb, 0 g Fib, 1 g Prot, 2 mg Calc. **POINTS** value: **1.**

Plan Ahead   The log of unbaked dough can be frozen up to 3 months. You can then cut off as many slices of the frozen dough as you like and freshly bake them. Be sure to add a few minutes to the baking time.

Linzer Sandwich Cookies

HANDS-ON PREP 35 MIN   COOK 8 MIN   MAKES 24

2   cups cake flour
1   teaspoon baking powder
1   teaspoon cinnamon
¼   teaspoon salt
¾   cup sugar
3   tablespoons unsalted butter, softened
2   tablespoons canola oil
1   teaspoon grated lemon zest
1   large egg

1   teaspoon vanilla extract
¼   cup hazelnuts, toasted, skinned, and chopped
½   cup boysenberry, apricot, or raspberry
    fruit spread

1 Whisk together the cake flour, baking powder, cinnamon, and salt in a medium bowl; set aside. With an electric mixer on low speed, beat the sugar, butter, oil, and lemon zest until light and fluffy. Beat in the egg and vanilla. Add the flour mixture and beat just until blended. Divide the dough in half. Shape each half into a ball, then flatten into a disk. Roll out each portion of dough between sheets of wax paper to ⅛-inch thickness. Refrigerate until cold, at least 1 hour or up to 2 days.

2 Meanwhile, place the oven racks in the upper and lower thirds of the oven and preheat the oven to 350°F. Spray 2 large baking sheets with nonstick spray.

3 Working with 1 sheet of dough (keep the remaining dough in the refrigerator), peel off the top sheet of wax paper, then place it back on the dough. Flip the dough over; remove the top sheet of wax paper. With a 2½-inch scalloped or round cookie cutter, cut out rounds from the dough. With a spatula, transfer the rounds to a baking sheet about 1 inch apart. If the dough becomes too soft to work with, return to refrigerator until firm. With a 1-inch round cookie cutter, cut out and remove the centers from half of the dough rounds. Reserve all the dough scraps. Place the baking sheet in the refrigerator. Repeat with the remaining dough and dough scraps.

4 Lightly brush the cookies with the cutout centers with water and sprinkle evenly with the hazelnuts. Bake the cookies until firm and lightly browned along the edges, 6–8 minutes for the cookies with the cutout centers and 8–10 minutes for the solid cookies, rotating the baking sheets halfway through the baking. With a spatula, transfer the cookies to racks and let cool completely. Brush the solid cookies with the fruit spread and top with the cutout cookies, making a total of 24 cookies.

PER SERVING (1 cookie): 117 Cal, 4 g Fat, 1 g Sat Fat, 0 g Trans Fat, 13 mg Chol, 49 mg Sod, 20 g Carb, 1 g Fib, 2 g Prot, 20 mg Calc. *POINTS* value: *2.*

Chocolate-Dipped Meringue Fingers

HANDS-ON PREP 20 MIN   COOK 1 HR   MAKES 30

2   teaspoons instant espresso powder
1   teaspoon unsweetened cocoa powder
2   egg whites, at room temperature
⅛   teaspoon cream of tartar
Pinch salt
½   cup superfine sugar
½   teaspoon vanilla extract
2   ounces bittersweet or semisweet
    chocolate, chopped

1 Preheat the oven to 225°F. Line a large baking sheet with parchment paper.

2 Sift together the espresso powder and cocoa powder into a small bowl; set aside. With an electric mixer on medium speed, beat the egg whites, cream of tartar, and salt in a medium bowl until soft peaks form. Increase the speed to medium-high. Add the superfine sugar, 1 tablespoon at a time, beating until stiff, glossy peaks form. Beat in the vanilla and espresso mixture just until blended.

3 Spoon the meringue into a pastry bag fitted with a ½-inch star tip. Pipe 3-inch-long x ¾-inch-wide meringue fingers onto the baking sheet about 1 inch apart, making a total of 30 meringues. Bake for 1 hour. Turn off the oven and leave the meringues in the oven until dry, at least 5 hours or up to overnight.

4 Put the chocolate in a small microwavable bowl. Microwave on Medium just until melted, 1–2 minutes, stirring at 30-second intervals. Stir until smooth, then let cool slightly. Dip one end of each meringue finger into the chocolate, allowing the excess to drip off. Place the meringues on a sheet of wax paper. Let stand until the chocolate sets, about 30 minutes.

PER SERVING (1 cookie): 24 Cal, 1 g Fat, 0 g Sat Fat, 0 g Trans Fat, 0 mg Chol, 13 mg Sod, 4 g Carb, 0 g Fib, 0 g Prot, 1 mg Calc. **POINTS** value: **1.**

Good Idea   If you don't have a pastry bag or star tip, you can drop small mounds of the meringue from a teaspoon onto the baking sheet. Smooth the tops of the meringues with a dampened finger if necessary. Or use a zip-close plastic bag with one corner snipped off and pipe small mounds.

Fig, Hazelnut, and White Chocolate Biscotti

HANDS-ON PREP 30 MIN   COOK 1 HR   MAKES 52

- ½ cup hazelnuts
- ½ cup sugar
- 2 large eggs
- 2 teaspoons grated orange zest
- 1 teaspoon vanilla extract
- 1¾ cups whole-wheat pastry flour
- ¾ teaspoon baking soda
- ¼ teaspoon salt
- ½ cup dried figs, stemmed and finely chopped
- 4 ounces white chocolate, chopped into ¼-inch pieces

1 Place the oven racks in the upper and lower thirds of the oven and preheat the oven to 300°F.

2 Spread the hazelnuts on a baking sheet. Bake until toasted, about 15 minutes. Wrap the hot hazelnuts in a clean kitchen towel and rub the nuts together to remove as much of the skins as possible. Let the nuts cool, then coarsely chop; set aside.

3 With an electric mixer on medium speed, beat the sugar, eggs, orange zest, and vanilla in a large bowl until slightly thickened, about 1 minute. Reduce the speed to low. Add the pastry flour, baking soda, and salt; beat until blended. Stir in the figs, chocolate, and hazelnuts.

4 Spray a baking sheet with nonstick spray. Generously flour a work surface. Divide the dough in half. Roll each half in the flour to coat, then roll each piece of dough into a 13-inch-long log (the dough will be soft). Transfer the logs to the baking sheet about 4 inches apart. Bake until firm to the touch, about 30 minutes. Let cool on the baking sheet on a rack about 30 minutes.

5 With a spatula, loosen each log from the baking sheet. With a serrated knife, cut each log crosswise into ½-inch-thick slices, making a total of 52 slices. Stand the slices on 2 baking sheets. Bake until dry, about 20 minutes, rotating the baking sheets halfway through the baking. Let cool completely on racks.

PER SERVING (1 biscotti): 52 Cal, 2 g Fat, 1 g Sat Fat, 0 g Trans Fat, 9 mg Chol, 37 mg Sod, 8 g Carb, 1 g Fib, 1 g Prot, 12 mg Calc. *POINTS* value: *1.*

Express Lane   To save time, look for chopped hazelnuts in the baking aisle of the supermarket. They will still need to be toasted, but you won't need to remove the skins.

Mini Chocolate Brownie Biscotti

HANDS-ON PREP 30 MIN   COOK 30 MIN   MAKES 56

2   cups all-purpose flour
¾   cup mini semisweet chocolate chips
½   cup Dutch-process cocoa
1   tablespoon instant espresso powder
1   teaspoon baking soda
¼   teaspoon salt
1   cup sugar
2   large eggs
2   egg whites
2   teaspoons vanilla extract
¾   cup walnuts, chopped

1 Place the oven racks in the upper and lower thirds of the oven and preheat the oven to 350°F. Line 2 large baking sheets with parchment paper.

2 Put the flour, ¼ cup of the chocolate chips, the cocoa, espresso powder, baking soda, and salt in a food processor; process until the chocolate is finely chopped, about 1 minute. Transfer to a large bowl. Put the sugar, eggs, egg whites, and vanilla in the food processor (no need to clean the bowl); process until the mixture is slightly thickened, about 1 minute. Add to the flour mixture along with the remaining ½ cup of chocolate chips and ½ cup of the walnuts; stir until blended.

3 Spoon the dough onto the baking sheets, forming two 14 x 1½-inch logs on each baking sheet, using ¾ cup dough for each log and placing about 5 inches apart. Sprinkle evenly with the remaining ¼ cup of walnuts, pressing them lightly so they adhere. Bake the logs until firm when lightly pressed, about 15 minutes, rotating the baking sheets halfway through the baking. Let cool on the baking sheets on racks about 15 minutes.

4 Meanwhile, reduce the oven temperature to 275°F.

5 With a narrow metal spatula, loosen the logs from the parchment paper. With a serrated knife, cut each log crosswise into ½-inch-thick slices, making a total of 56 slices. Stand the slices on the baking sheets. Bake until dry, 15–20 minutes, rotating the baking sheets halfway through the baking. With a spatula, transfer the biscotti to racks and let cool completely.

PER SERVING (2 biscotti): 62 Cal, 2 g Fat, 0 g Sat Fat, 0 g Trans Fat, 8 mg Chol, 40 mg Sod, 10 g Carb, 0 g Fib, 2 g Prot, 6 mg Calc. **POINTS** value: *1.*

Quick Breads

Chapter 4

Banana-Coconut Bread

HANDS-ON PREP 20 MIN   COOK 55 MIN   SERVES 12

2½ cups all-purpose flour

2   teaspoons baking powder

1   teaspoon baking soda

½   teaspoon salt

¾   cup sugar

3   egg whites

½   cup unsweetened applesauce

2   tablespoons canola oil

4   very ripe medium bananas, mashed (2 cups)

½   cup diced mixed dried tropical fruit

⅓   cup + 2 tablespoons unsweetened flaked coconut

1 Preheat the oven to 375°F. Spray a 5 x 9-inch loaf pan with nonstick spray.

2 Whisk together the flour, baking powder, baking soda, and salt in a large bowl. Whisk together the sugar, egg whites, applesauce, and oil in a medium bowl. Add the applesauce mixture, bananas, dried fruit, and ⅓ cup of the coconut to the flour mixture; stir just until moistened.

3 Scrape the batter into the pan; sprinkle with the remaining 2 tablespoons of coconut. Bake until a toothpick inserted into the center comes out clean, 55–60 minutes. Let cool in the pan on a rack 10 minutes. Remove the bread from the pan and let cool completely on the rack. Wrap the cooled bread in plastic wrap; let stand overnight before slicing for the neatest slices.

PER SERVING (1/12 of loaf): 241 Cal, 5 g Fat, 2 g Sat Fat, 0 g Trans Fat, 0 mg Chol, 301 mg Sod, 47 g Carb, 3 g Fib, 4 g Prot, 56 mg Calc. **POINTS** value: **5.**

How We Did It   For the best flavor and texture in this quick bread, use bananas that are completely covered with brown spots. Diced tropical fruit is a combination of various fruits such as dried pineapple, mango, and papaya. They can be found packaged in bags near the raisins or in the produce section in supermarkets. If you can't find it, you can buy the different dried fruits separately and dice them yourself.

Chocolate-Gingerbread Loaf

HANDS-ON PREP 15 MIN   COOK 50 MIN   SERVES 16

2   cups all-purpose flour
2   teaspoons ground ginger
1   teaspoon cinnamon
1   teaspoon baking soda
¼   teaspoon salt
½   cup mini semisweet chocolate chips
¼   cup crystallized ginger, finely chopped
¾   cup dark molasses

½   cup packed light brown sugar
¼   cup canola oil
1   large egg
½   cup hot water

1 Preheat the oven to 350°F. Spray a 5 x 9-inch loaf pan with nonstick spray.

2 Whisk together the flour, ground ginger, cinnamon, baking soda, and salt in a large bowl. Stir in the chocolate chips and crystallized ginger. Whisk together the molasses, brown sugar, oil, and egg in a medium bowl. Whisk in the hot water until blended. Add the molasses mixture to the flour mixture; stir until well blended.

3 Pour the batter into the pan. Bake until a toothpick inserted into the center comes out clean, about 50 minutes. Let cool in the pan on a rack 15 minutes. Remove the bread from the pan and let cool completely on the rack.

PER SERVING (¹⁄₁₆ of loaf): 201 Cal, 5 g Fat, 1 g Sat Fat, 0 g Trans Fat, 14 mg Chol, 135 mg Sod, 36 g Carb, 1 g Fib, 2 g Prot, 55 mg Calc. **POINTS** value: **4.**

How We Did It   Crystallized ginger can get a bit sticky when chopped, so we like to first spray the knife with nonstick spray, which keeps the ginger from sticking to the blade.

Carrot, Zucchini, and Walnut Bread

HANDS-ON PREP 25 MIN   COOK 50 MIN   SERVES 16

1½ cups whole-wheat flour

1   cup all-purpose flour

1½ teaspoons cinnamon

1   teaspoon baking powder

1   teaspoon baking soda

½   teaspoon salt

¾   cup plain fat-free yogurt

½   cup packed light brown sugar

½   cup unsweetened applesauce

¼   cup canola oil

2   large egg whites

4   small carrots, shredded (about 1½ cups)

1   small zucchini, shredded (about 1 cup)

½   cup walnuts, chopped

1 Preheat the oven to 350°F. Spray a 5 x 9-inch loaf pan with nonstick spray.

2 Whisk together the whole-wheat flour, all-purpose flour, cinnamon, baking powder, baking soda, and salt in a large bowl. Whisk together the yogurt, brown sugar, applesauce, oil, and egg whites in a medium bowl. Add the applesauce mixture to the flour mixture; stir just until the flour mixture is moistened. Stir in the carrots, zucchini, and walnuts just until blended.

3 Scrape the batter into the pan. Bake until a toothpick inserted into the center comes out clean, 50–60 minutes. Let cool in the pan on a rack 10 minutes. Remove the bread from the pan and let cool completely on the rack.

PER SERVING (¹⁄₁₆ of loaf): 159 Cal, 6 g Fat, 1 g Sat Fat, 0 g Trans Fat, 0 mg Chol, 207 mg Sod, 24 g Carb, 2 g Fib, 4 g Prot, 60 mg Calc. *POINTS* value: *3.*

Good Idea   This moist, not-too-sweet bread is a good make-ahead choice, as it will last, tightly wrapped, up to 3 days at room temperature or up to 1 week if refrigerated.

CARROT, ZUCCHINI,
AND WALNUT BREAD

Double Cranberry–Orange Loaf

HANDS-ON PREP 20 MIN   COOK 50 MIN   SERVES 12

1 cup all-purpose flour
1 cup whole-wheat flour
⅔ cup sugar
1½ teaspoons baking powder
½ teaspoon baking soda
½ teaspoon salt
1 tablespoon grated orange zest
   (about 1 orange)
1 cup fresh orange juice

3 tablespoons canola oil
1 large egg
1 cup fresh or frozen cranberries
½ cup dried cranberries

1 Preheat the oven to 350°F. Spray a 5 x 9-inch loaf pan with nonstick spray.

2 Whisk together the all-purpose flour, whole-wheat flour, sugar, baking powder, baking soda, and salt in a large bowl. Whisk together the orange zest and juice, oil, and egg in a medium bowl. Add the orange juice mixture, fresh cranberries, and dried cranberries to the flour mixture; stir just until the flour mixture is moistened.

3 Scrape the batter into the pan. Bake until a toothpick inserted into the center comes out clean, 50–60 minutes. Let cool in the pan on a rack 10 minutes. Remove the loaf from the pan and let cool completely on the rack. Wrap the cooled loaf in plastic wrap; let stand overnight at room temperature before slicing for the neatest slices.

PER SERVING (1/12 of loaf): 180 Cal, 4 g Fat, 0 g Sat Fat, 0 g Trans Fat, 18 mg Chol, 219 mg Sod, 34 g Carb, 2 g Fib, 3 g Prot, 44 mg Calc. *POINTS* value: *4.*

Good Idea   It's a good idea to freeze a few bags of cranberries when they are readily available in the fall and early winter so you have them on hand to use during the year. If you are using frozen cranberries, stir them into the batter while still frozen.

Chocolate Streusel Coffee Cake

HANDS-ON PREP 20 MIN   COOK 25 MIN   SERVES 16

STREUSEL

½ cup packed light brown sugar

2 tablespoons unsweetened cocoa powder

2 teaspoons canola oil

½ teaspoon cinnamon

½ cup semisweet chocolate chips

CAKE

2¼ cups whole-wheat pastry flour

¾ cup granulated sugar

1½ teaspoons baking powder

½ teaspoon baking soda

½ teaspoon salt

1 cup plain low-fat yogurt

2 large eggs

¼ cup canola oil

½ teaspoon almond extract

½ cup dried tart cherries, coarsely chopped

3 tablespoons sliced almonds

1 Preheat the oven to 350°F. Spray a 9 x 13-inch baking pan with nonstick spray.

2 To make the streusel, with your fingers, rub together the brown sugar, cocoa, oil, and cinnamon in a small bowl until well blended. Stir in the chocolate chips; set aside.

3 To make the cake, whisk together the pastry flour, granulated sugar, baking powder, baking soda, and salt in a large bowl. Whisk together the yogurt, eggs, oil, and almond extract in a medium bowl. Add the yogurt mixture and cherries to the flour mixture; stir just until the flour mixture is moistened.

4 Spoon half of the batter into the pan; spread evenly (the layer will be thin). Sprinkle with half of the streusel. Spoon the remaining batter over the streusel and spread gently (it doesn't have to cover completely). Sprinkle evenly with the remaining streusel and the almonds. Bake until a toothpick inserted into the center comes out clean, about 25 minutes. Let cool in the pan on a rack 30 minutes. Serve warm.

PER SERVING (¹⁄₁₆ of cake): 219 Cal, 7 g Fat, 2 g Sat Fat, 0 g Trans Fat, 27 mg Chol, 183 mg Sod, 37 g Carb, 3 g Fib, 5 g Prot, 79 mg Calc. *POINTS* value: *4.*

Try It Whole-wheat pastry flour is made from soft wheat that is very finely ground, making it ideal for cakes, cookies, and pastries, while regular whole-wheat flour is milled from hard winter wheat, which is higher in gluten, making it ideal for bread and rolls. In whole-wheat pastry flour, part of the bran and germ portion remains, so baked goods are more nutritious than those made with white pastry flour. It is available in health food and specialty food stores.

Apple-Cranberry Coffee Cake

HANDS-ON PREP 15 MIN   COOK 30 MIN   SERVES 12

¾ cup sugar

1½ teaspoons cinnamon

2 cups all-purpose flour

2 teaspoons baking powder

1 teaspoon baking soda

½ teaspoon salt

1 cup plain fat-free yogurt

¼ cup canola oil

1 large egg

1½ teaspoons vanilla extract

2 Granny Smith or Golden Delicious apples, peeled, cored, and cut into ½-inch pieces (about 2 cups)

½ cup fresh or frozen cranberries, coarsely chopped

1 Preheat the oven to 375°F. Spray a 9-inch square baking pan with nonstick spray.

2 Stir together 2 tablespoons of the sugar and ½ teaspoon of the cinnamon in a cup; set aside.

3 Whisk together the flour, the remaining sugar, the baking powder, baking soda, the remaining 1 teaspoon of cinnamon, and the salt in a large bowl. Whisk together the yogurt, oil, egg, and vanilla in a medium bowl. Add the yogurt mixture, apples, and cranberries to the flour mixture; stir just until blended.

4 Spoon the batter into the pan; spread evenly. Sprinkle evenly with the reserved cinnamon sugar. Bake until a toothpick inserted into the center comes out clean, 30–35 minutes. Let cool completely in the pan on a rack. Cover with plastic wrap and let stand at least 6 hours before slicing for the neatest slices.

PER SERVING (1/12 of cake): 197 Cal, 5 g Fat, 1 g Sat Fat, 0 g Trans Fat, 18 mg Chol, 306 mg Sod, 34 g Carb, 1 g Fib, 4 g Prot, 96 mg Calc. **POINTS** value: **4.**

How We Did It   You can use either Granny Smith or Golden Delicious apples in the cake. If you prefer a sweeter taste, use Golden Delicious apples, and if you like a little more tartness, use Granny Smiths.

Streusel-Topped Apple-Spice Muffins

HANDS-ON PREP 15 MIN   COOK 15 MIN   SERVES 12

STREUSEL TOPPING

3   tablespoons all-purpose flour

3   tablespoons packed light brown sugar

1   tablespoon canola oil

½   teaspoon apple pie spice or cinnamon

MUFFINS

2   cups all-purpose flour

2   teaspoons baking powder

1   teaspoon apple pie spice or cinnamon

½   teaspoon baking soda

¼   teaspoon salt

½   cup packed light brown sugar

½   cup unsweetened applesauce

½   cup plain fat-free yogurt

2   tablespoons canola oil

2   tablespoons unsalted butter, melted

1   large egg

1   Granny Smith apple, peeled, cored, and chopped (about 1 cup)

1 Preheat the oven to 400°F. Line a 12-cup muffin pan with paper liners.

2 To make the streusel, combine the streusel ingredients in a small bowl until moistened; set aside.

3 To make the muffins, whisk together the flour, baking powder, apple pie spice, baking soda, and salt in a large bowl. Whisk together the brown sugar, applesauce, yogurt, oil, melted butter, and egg in a medium bowl. Add the applesauce mixture and apple to the flour mixture; stir just until the flour mixture is moistened.

4 Fill the muffin cups evenly with the batter. Sprinkle evenly with the streusel, pressing lightly so it adheres. Bake until a toothpick inserted into the center of a muffin comes out clean, 15–20 minutes. Let cool in the pan on a rack 5 minutes. Remove the muffins from the pan and let cool on a rack about 15 minutes longer. Serve warm.

PER SERVING (1 muffin): 206 Cal, 6 g Fat, 2 g Sat Fat, 0 g Trans Fat, 23 mg Chol, 202 mg Sod, 35 g Carb, 1 g Fib, 4 g Prot, 87 mg Calc. **POINTS** value: **4.**

How We Did It   When making muffins, you want to gently combine the liquid mixture and flour mixture just until the flour mixture is moistened and there are no streaks of flour remaining. If the batter is mixed more than this, the muffins will be tough.

OLD-FASHIONED SOUR CREAM
COFFEE CAKE

Old-Fashioned Sour Cream Coffee Cake

HANDS-ON PREP 25 MIN   COOK 40 MIN   SERVES 16

½ cup pecans, chopped
½ cup packed light brown sugar
2 teaspoons cinnamon
1½ cups whole-wheat pastry flour
1 cup all-purpose flour
2 teaspoons baking powder
½ teaspoon baking soda
½ teaspoon salt
4 tablespoons unsalted butter, softened
1⅓ cups granulated sugar

2 large eggs
2 egg whites
1¼ cups fat-free sour cream
2 teaspoons vanilla extract

1 Preheat the oven to 350°F. Spray a 10-inch Bundt pan with nonstick spray.

2 Evenly sprinkle 2 tablespoons of the pecans in the bottom of the pan. Combine the remaining pecans, the brown sugar, and cinnamon in a small bowl; set aside. Whisk together the pastry flour, all-purpose flour, baking powder, baking soda, and salt in a medium bowl; set aside.

3 With an electric mixer on medium speed, beat the butter and ⅓ cup of the granulated sugar in a large bowl until light and fluffy, about 2 minutes. Gradually beat in the remaining 1 cup of granulated sugar, then beat 1 more minute. Beat in the eggs and egg whites, one at a time, beating well after each addition. Beat in the sour cream and vanilla. Reduce the speed to low. Gradually add the flour mixture, beating just until blended.

4 Spoon one-third of the batter into the pan; spread evenly. Sprinkle evenly with half of the reserved brown sugar mixture. Spoon half of the remaining batter on top; spread evenly. Sprinkle with the remaining brown sugar mixture. Spoon the remaining batter on top; spread evenly. Bake until a toothpick inserted into the center comes out clean, 40–45 minutes. Let cool in the pan on a rack 10 minutes. Remove the cake from the pan and let cool completely on the rack.

PER SERVING (⅟₁₆ of cake): 233 Cal, 6 g Fat, 2 g Sat Fat, 0 g Trans Fat, 36 mg Chol, 219 mg Sod, 42 g Carb, 2 g Fib, 5 g Prot, 78 mg Calc. **POINTS** value: **5.**

How We Did It   When sprinkling the brown sugar mixture over the batter, keep it away from the side of the pan so it doesn't stick to the pan when baked.

Maple-Raisin Bran Muffins

HANDS-ON PREP 15 MIN   COOK 20 MIN   SERVES 12

1½ cups whole bran cereal (not flakes)
½ cup raisins
¼ cup light olive oil
½ cup boiling water
1 cup low-fat buttermilk
¼ cup pure maple syrup
1 large egg
1⅓ cups whole-wheat pastry flour
1¼ teaspoons baking soda
¼ teaspoon salt
½ cup walnuts, chopped

1 Toss together the cereal, raisins, and oil in a large bowl until moistened. Pour the boiling water over the cereal mixture and toss to evenly moisten; let cool slightly.

2 Add the buttermilk, maple syrup, and egg to the cereal mixture; stir until mixed well. Whisk together the pastry flour, baking soda, and salt in a small bowl. Add the flour mixture and walnuts to the cereal mixture and stir just until the flour mixture is moistened. Cover the bowl with plastic wrap; let stand 15 minutes.

3 Meanwhile, preheat the oven to 400°F. Line a 12-cup muffin pan with paper liners.

4 Fill the muffin cups evenly with the batter. Bake until a toothpick inserted into the center comes out clean, 20–25 minutes. Let cool in the pan on a rack 10 minutes. Remove the muffins from the pan and let cool completely on the rack.

PER SERVING (1 muffin): 182 Cal, 9 g Fat, 1 g Sat Fat, 0 g Trans Fat, 18 mg Chol, 228 mg Sod, 26 g Carb, 4 g Fib, 5 g Prot, 72 mg Calc. **POINTS** value: **4.**

Food Note Light olive oil has a neutral flavor, so it can be used in place of canola oil in this and in most other baking recipes.

Lemon-Poppy Seed Mini-Muffins

HANDS-ON PREP 15 MIN   COOK 10 MIN   SERVES 24

2   cups all-purpose flour
1   cup sugar
3   tablespoons poppy seeds
2½ teaspoons baking powder
½   teaspoon salt
¾   cup fat-free milk
¼   cup canola oil
1   large egg
1   egg white
1   tablespoon grated lemon zest (about 2 lemons)
¼   cup fresh lemon juice

1 Preheat the oven to 400°F. Line a 24-cup mini-muffin pan with paper liners.

2 Whisk together the flour, ¾ cup of the sugar, the poppy seeds, baking powder, and salt in a large bowl. Whisk together the milk, oil, egg, egg white, and lemon zest in a small bowl. Add the milk mixture to the flour mixture and stir just until the flour mixture is moistened.

3 Fill the muffin cups evenly with the batter. Bake until the tops spring back when lightly pressed, 10–15 minutes. Let cool in the pan on a rack.

4 Meanwhile, combine the remaining ¼ cup of sugar and the lemon juice in a small microwavable bowl. Microwave on High until it boils, 45 seconds to 1 minute; stir until the sugar is dissolved. With a wooden skewer, poke 5 holes in each muffin. Gradually brush the lemon syrup over the muffins, letting it soak in before brushing on more syrup. Serve the muffins warm or let cool completely.

PER SERVING (1 muffin): 104 Cal, 3 g Fat, 0 g Sat Fat, 0 g Trans Fat, 9 mg Chol, 109 mg Sod, 17 g Carb, 0 g Fib, 2 g Prot, 57 mg Calc. *POINTS* value: *2.*

How We Did It The lemon syrup adds both flavor and moisture to the muffins. Poking holes in the muffins and brushing them while warm ensures that they will absorb every bit of the delectable sweet-tart syrup.

BLUEBERRY-CORN
MUFFINS AND
MAPLE-RAISIN
BRAN MUFFINS, PAGE 100

Blueberry-Corn Muffins

HANDS-ON PREP 10 MIN   COOK 15 MIN   SERVES 12

1½ cups all-purpose flour

½ cup cornmeal

6   tablespoons sugar

1½ teaspoons baking powder

½ teaspoon baking soda

¼ teaspoon salt

1½ cups fresh or frozen blueberries

1   cup low-fat buttermilk

3   tablespoons canola oil

1   large egg

1   tablespoon grated lemon zest (about 2 lemons)

1 Preheat the oven to 400°F. Line a 12-cup muffin pan with paper liners.

2 Whisk together the flour, cornmeal, 5 tablespoons of the sugar, the baking powder, baking soda, and salt in a large bowl. Gently stir in the blueberries. Whisk together the buttermilk, oil, egg, and lemon zest in a small bowl. Add the buttermilk mixture to the flour mixture and stir just until the flour mixture is moistened.

3 Fill the muffin cups evenly with the batter and sprinkle evenly with the remaining 1 tablespoon of sugar. Bake until the muffins spring back when lightly pressed, 15–20 minutes. Let cool in the pan on a rack 5 minutes. Remove the muffins from the pan and let cool on the rack about 15 minutes longer. Serve warm.

PER SERVING (1 muffin): 158 Cal, 4 g Fat, 1 g Sat Fat, 0 g Trans Fat, 18 mg Chol, 190 mg Sod, 27 g Carb, 1 g Fib, 3 g Prot, 64 mg Calc. **POINTS** value: **3.**

Express Lane Up to several hours ahead, prepare the buttermilk mixture and refrigerate. Prepare the flour mixture (leave out the berries) and set aside at room temperature. Just before baking, add the blueberries to the flour mixture, then proceed as directed in the recipe.

Dried Blueberry Breakfast Scones

HANDS-ON PREP 15 MIN   COOK 15 MIN   SERVES 12

1½ cups whole-wheat pastry flour

½ cup quick-cooking (not instant) oats

¼ cup ground flaxseed

¼ cup packed light brown sugar

1½ teaspoons baking powder

½ teaspoon baking soda

¼ teaspoon salt

3 tablespoons cold unsalted butter, cut into pieces

¾ cup dried blueberries

¾ cup low-fat buttermilk

1 egg white

1 tablespoon turbinado (raw) sugar

1 Preheat the oven to 375°F. Spray a baking sheet with nonstick spray.

2 Whisk together the pastry flour, oats, flaxseed, brown sugar, baking powder, baking soda, and salt in a large bowl. With a pastry blender or 2 knives used scissor-fashion, cut in the butter until the mixture resembles fine crumbs with some small pieces of butter remaining. Gently stir in the blueberries. Set aside 1 tablespoon of the buttermilk. Whisk together the remaining buttermilk and the egg white in a small bowl. Add to the flour mixture and stir just until the flour mixture is moistened (the dough will be soft).

3 Gather the dough into a ball and place on a lightly floured surface; divide in half. Knead each portion 2 times. Place the 2 pieces of dough on the baking sheet 5 inches apart. Pat each piece of dough into a 6-inch round. Spray a long, thin knife with nonstick spray; cut each round into 6 wedges (do not separate the wedges).

4 Brush the scones with the reserved buttermilk and sprinkle evenly with the turbinado sugar. Bake until a toothpick inserted into the center comes out clean, 15–20 minutes. Let cool on the baking sheet on a rack 5 minutes. With a pancake spatula, slide each round onto a rack and let cool completely. Separate the wedges.

PER SERVING (1 scone): 153 Cal, 5 g Fat, 2 g Sat Fat, 0 g Trans Fat, 8 mg Chol, 188 mg Sod, 26 g Carb, 4 g Fib, 4 g Prot, 72 mg Calc. **POINTS** value: **3.**

Food Note   Turbinado sugar is raw sugar that has been steam-cleaned. Its slightly coarse, pale amber crystals have a subtle molasses flavor.

Chocolate Chip–Orange Scones

HANDS-ON PREP 20 MIN   COOK 10 MIN   SERVES 24

2   cups all-purpose flour

¼   cup sugar

1   teaspoon baking powder

¼   teaspoon baking soda

¼   teaspoon salt

3   tablespoons cold unsalted butter, cut into pieces

½   cup mini semisweet chocolate chips

¾   cup low-fat buttermilk

1   large egg

1   tablespoon grated orange zest (about 1 orange)

1   cup confectioners' sugar

4   teaspoons fresh orange juice

1 Preheat the oven to 400°F. Spray a large baking sheet with nonstick spray.

2 Whisk together the flour, sugar, baking powder, baking soda, and salt in a large bowl. With a pastry blender or 2 knives used scissor-fashion, cut in the butter until the mixture resembles fine crumbs with some small pieces of butter remaining. Stir in the chocolate chips. Whisk together the buttermilk, egg, and orange zest in a small bowl. Add to the flour mixture and stir just until a dough forms.

3 Gather the dough into a ball and place on a lightly floured surface. Lightly knead 2 times. With a floured rolling pin, roll the dough to ¾-inch thickness. With a 1½-inch round cookie cutter, cut out rounds, dipping the cutter into flour between cuts to prevent sticking. Place the scones on the baking sheet about 1 inch apart. Gently gather the scraps; reroll and cut out more scones, making a total of 24 scones. Bake until golden brown, 10–12 minutes. Let cool on the baking sheet on a rack until warm, about 10 minutes.

4 Stir together the confectioners' sugar and orange juice in a small bowl until smooth. Place a sheet of wax paper under a rack. Dip the tops of the scones in the glaze; place, glaze side up, on the rack. Let stand until the glaze sets, about 1 hour.

PER SERVING (1 scone): 104 Cal, 3 g Fat, 2 g Sat Fat, 0 g Trans Fat, 14 mg Chol, 72 mg Sod, 18 g Carb, 0 g Fib, 2 g Prot, 30 mg Calc. *POINTS* value: *2.*

Plan Ahead   These scones are great for making ahead. Place the unglazed scones in a zip-close plastic bag and freeze. To serve, let thaw at room temperature, then prepare the glaze and dip the tops.

Berry Shortcakes

HANDS-ON PREP 30 MIN   COOK 12 MIN   SERVES 12

SHORTCAKES

½ cup sugar

2 cups all-purpose flour

2 teaspoons baking powder

½ teaspoon salt

¼ teaspoon baking soda

¾ cup low-fat buttermilk

3 tablespoons canola oil

1 large egg

1½ teaspoons grated lemon zest

1½ cups blueberries

FILLING AND TOPPING

2 (1-pound) containers strawberries, hulled and sliced

⅓ cup sugar

2 (6-ounce) containers raspberries

1½ cups thawed frozen fat-free whipped topping

1 cup plain fat-free Greek-style yogurt

1 Preheat the oven to 400°F. Spray a large baking sheet with nonstick spray.

2 To make the shortcakes, reserve 1 tablespoon of the sugar. Whisk together the flour, the remaining sugar, the baking powder, salt, and baking soda in a large bowl. Whisk together the buttermilk, oil, egg, and lemon zest in a medium bowl. Add the buttermilk mixture and blueberries to the flour mixture; stir just until the flour mixture is moistened (the dough will be soft).

3 Turn the dough out onto a floured surface; turn to coat with the flour. Lightly knead 2 times. With a floured rolling pin, roll the dough into a ¾-inch-thick square. Lightly spray a long, thin knife with nonstick spray. Cut the dough into 12 squares. Place the shortcakes on the baking sheet about 1 inch apart; sprinkle with the reserved 1 tablespoon of sugar. Bake until the tops spring back when lightly pressed, about 12 minutes. Transfer the shortcakes to a rack and let cool.

4 To make the filling and topping, combine the strawberries and sugar in a large bowl. Let stand 15 minutes to allow the juices to form; gently stir in the raspberries. Fold together the whipped topping and yogurt in a medium bowl just until combined.

5 Split the shortcakes. Place the bottom halves of the shortcakes on plates and top evenly with the strawberry mixture and yogurt topping. Cover with the tops of the shortcakes. Serve at once.

PER SERVING (1 shortcake, ½ cup berries, and scant ¼ cup topping): 240 Cal, 5 g Fat, 1 g Sat Fat, 0 g Trans Fat, 19 mg Chol, 247 mg Sod, 46 g Carb, 4 g Fib, 5 g Prot, 127 mg Calc. **POINTS** value: **4.**

How We Did It   The key to tender, delicate scones is a light touch. Stir the ingredients together just enough to form a soft dough. A quick kneading is all that's necessary to bring the dough together nicely.

BERRY SHORTCAKES

Caramelized Apple-Filled Cinnamon Shortcake

HANDS-ON PREP 30 MIN   COOK 40 MIN   SERVES 12

SHORTCAKE

1½ cups whole-wheat pastry flour

½ cup packed light brown sugar

2 teaspoons cinnamon

1½ teaspoons baking powder

¼ teaspoon baking soda

¼ teaspoon salt

½ cup fat-free milk

2 tablespoons unsalted butter, melted

1 large egg

¼ cup pecans, chopped

1 tablespoon granulated sugar

FILLING

1 tablespoon unsalted butter

6 large Golden Delicious apples, peeled, cored, and sliced (about 8 cups)

¼ cup granulated sugar

1½ pints vanilla fat-free frozen yogurt

1 Preheat the oven to 375°F. Spray a 9-inch round baking pan with nonstick spray.

2 To make the shortcake, whisk together the pastry flour, brown sugar, 1¾ teaspoons of the cinnamon, the baking powder, baking soda, and salt in a large bowl. Whisk together the milk, melted butter, and egg in a small bowl. Add the milk mixture to the flour mixture and stir just until the flour mixture is moistened.

3 Scrape the batter into the pan and spread evenly; sprinkle evenly with the pecans. Combine the granulated sugar and the remaining ¼ teaspoon of cinnamon in a small bowl; sprinkle over the batter. Bake until a toothpick inserted into the center comes out clean, about 20 minutes. Let cool in the pan on a rack 10 minutes. Remove from the pan and let cool completely on the rack.

4 To make the filling, melt the butter in a very large nonstick skillet over medium heat. Add the apples and cook, stirring frequently, until beginning to soften, about 10 minutes. Stir in the granulated sugar and cook, stirring frequently, until the apples brown and soften, about 10 minutes. Remove the skillet from the heat and let cool 5 minutes.

5 With a serrated knife, cut the shortcake horizontally in half. Place the shortcake bottom, cut side up, on a serving plate. Spoon the apples on top of the shortcake and cover with the top of the shortcake. Cut into 12 wedges. Put each wedge on a plate and place a scoop of frozen yogurt alongside. Serve at once.

PER SERVING (¹⁄₁₂ of shortcake, and ¼ cup frozen yogurt): 258 Cal, 5 g Fat, 2 g Sat Fat, 0 g Trans Fat, 27 mg Chol, 191 mg Sod, 50 g Carb, 4 g Fib, 6 g Prot, 154 mg Calc. **POINTS** value: **5.**

Zap It   The microwave is the perfect place to quickly and easily melt butter. Place the butter in a glass measuring cup and microwave on High until melted, about 30 seconds.

Fruit
Desserts

Chapter 5

Apple Cider–Baked Apples

HANDS-ON PREP 20 MIN   COOK 45 MIN   SERVES 4

4   small McIntosh apples (5 ounces each)
3   tablespoons fresh lemon juice
4   tablespoons packed light brown sugar
1   tablespoon unsalted butter, softened
3   tablespoons apple cider or juice
4   (3-inch) cinnamon sticks
Apple leaves, for garnish (optional)

1 Preheat the oven to 450°F.

2 With a melon baller, cut out the apple cores without cutting all the way through the apples. Peel the apples and brush with the lemon juice to prevent browning. If necessary, cut a thin slice off the bottoms of the apples so they stand upright. Cut each apple crosswise into 1/4-inch-thick slices, then reassemble the slices to re-form each apple.

3 Stir together 2 tablespoons of the brown sugar and the butter in a small bowl. Stir together the remaining 2 tablespoons of brown sugar and the apple cider in another small bowl. Place the apples in a pie plate; fill the cavities with the butter mixture, then pour the cider mixture on top. Bake, basting 3 times, about 25 minutes.

4 Reduce the oven temperature to 350°F. Place the cinnamon sticks in the cavities of the apples. Bake, basting 3 more times, until the apples are tender and the juices are thick and syrupy, about 20 minutes. Transfer an apple to each of 4 plates and spoon the syrup over. Garnish with apple leaves (if using) and serve at once.

PER SERVING (1 apple): 143 Cal, 3 g Fat, 2 g Sat Fat, 0 g Trans Fat, 8 mg Chol, 9 mg Sod, 31 g Carb, 2 g Fib, 0 g Prot, 22 mg Calc. **POINTS** value: *3.*

Try It   During the fall apple-picking season, try to find some apple leaves; they make a lovely garnish. Just be sure to wash them thoroughly with warm, soapy water.

Sour Cherry Soup

HANDS-ON PREP 15 MIN   COOK: NONE   SERVES 4

1   (24-ounce) jar pitted tart cherries
2   teaspoons fresh lemon juice
Pinch salt
1   cup lime sorbet

1 Put the cherries in a sieve set over a medium bowl. Remove ½ cup of the cherries and set aside; reserve the juice. Put the remaining cherries in a food processor and puree until smooth. Pour the cherry puree through a sieve set over the same bowl, pressing hard on the solids to extract as much liquid as possible. Stir in the reserved cherry juice, the lemon juice, and salt.

2 Refrigerate, covered, until the soup is thoroughly chilled, at least 2 hours or up to 1 day. Ladle ½ cup soup into each of 4 shallow soup bowls. Garnish each serving with 2 tablespoons of the reserved cherries and a ¼-cup scoop of the sorbet. Serve at once.

PER SERVING (½ cup soup, 2 tablespoons cherries, and ¼ cup sorbet): 157 Cal, 0 g Fat, 0 g Sat Fat, 0 g Trans Fat, 0 mg Chol, 81 mg Sod, 41 g Carb, 3 g Fib, 2 g Prot, 26 mg Calc. *POINTS* value: *3.*

How We Did It An excellent, efficient straining technique is to use one rubber spatula to press the cherries through the sieve and another across the bottom of the sieve to help loosen the pulp that has been pushed through.

Double Berry Summer Pudding

HANDS-ON PREP 25 MIN   COOK 10 MIN   SERVES 6

- 2   pints blueberries
- ⅓ cup sugar
- 2   tablespoons water
- 2   cups chopped strawberries (about 14 strawberries)
- ½ teaspoon vanilla extract
- 10 slices day-old firm-textured white bread, crusts removed
- Mixed berries (optional)

1 Combine the blueberries, sugar, and water in a large saucepan and set over medium heat. Cook, stirring, until the berries begin to release their liquid, about 3 minutes. Bring to a boil over medium-high heat. Cook, stirring occasionally, until slightly thickened, about 5 minutes. Remove the saucepan from the heat and stir in the strawberries and vanilla.

2 Line a 2-quart bowl with 2 pieces of overlapping plastic wrap, allowing the excess to extend over the rim of the bowl by 4 inches. Line the bottom and side of the bowl with the bread, cutting it to fit as needed. Spoon the berry mixture into the bowl and smooth the top. Cover with a layer of bread, cutting it to fit as needed. Fold the plastic wrap over the top of the pudding. Place a plate, slightly smaller than the bowl, on top of the pudding and weight it down with about 4 cans of food. Refrigerate at least 8 hours or up to 2 days.

3 Fold back the plastic wrap and invert the pudding onto a serving plate. Lift off the bowl and remove the plastic wrap. Cut the pudding into wedges or spoon into bowls. Spoon mixed berries (if using) around each serving.

PER SERVING (1 cup pudding without mixed berries): 205 Cal, 2 g Fat, 0 g Sat Fat, 0 g Trans Fat, 0 mg Chol, 229 mg Sod, 46 g Carb, 4 g Fib, 4 g Prot, 65 mg Calc. **POINTS** value: *3.*

Try It   Replace 1 pint of the blueberries with 2 (6-ounce) containers of raspberries. Stir them into the cooked blueberries along with the strawberries and vanilla.

DOUBLE BERRY
SUMMER PUDDING

Clementines with Cardamom and Pistachios

HANDS-ON PREP 15 MIN   COOK 8 MIN   SERVES 4

½ **cup water**
¼ **cup sugar**
1 **(3-inch) cinnamon stick**
2 **(2½-inch-long) strips lemon zest, removed with a vegetable peeler**
3 **green cardamom pods, crushed**
4 **clementines, peeled, halved crosswise, and seeded**
1 **tablespoon finely chopped pistachios**

1 Put the water, sugar, cinnamon stick, lemon zest, and cardamom in a medium saucepan and set over high heat. Bring to a boil, stirring until the sugar is dissolved. Cook until slightly thickened, about 4 minutes.

2 Arrange the clementine halves, cut side up, in an 8-inch square baking dish or casserole. Pour the hot syrup over the clementines and set aside until room temperature, at least 2 hours or up to 8 hours.

3 Arrange 2 clementine halves in each of 4 serving dishes and sprinkle with the pistachios.

PER SERVING (1 clementine with syrup and scant 1 teaspoon pistachios): 95 Cal, 1 g Fat, 0 g Sat Fat, 0 g Trans Fat, 0 mg Chol, 1 mg Sod, 22 g Carb, 2 g Fib, 1 g Prot, 27 mg Calc. **POINTS** value: **2.**

Food Note Clementines are a cross between a mandarin and a sour orange. They are available in supermarkets from October through March and are appreciated for their deep orange color, lack of seeds, and delectably sweet flavor. Your best buy is usually to purchase them by the case.

Fresh Mandarin Gelatin

HANDS-ON PREP 15 MIN   COOK: NONE   SERVES 6

3 tablespoons unflavored gelatin (about
   4 envelopes)
1 cup water
5 cups strained fresh mandarin or
   tangerine juice
¼ cup packed light brown sugar

1 Lightly spray a 6-cup decorative mold with nonstick spray.

2 Sprinkle the gelatin over the water in a small bowl. Let stand until softened, about 5 minutes. Place the bowl in a larger bowl of hot water and stir until the gelatin is completely dissolved.

3 Whisk together the mandarin juice and brown sugar in a large bowl until the sugar is dissolved; whisk in the gelatin mixture. Pour through a fine-mesh sieve set over a large bowl, pressing hard on the solids to extract as much liquid as possible. Pour the strained mixture into the mold. Refrigerate, covered, until thoroughly chilled and set, at least 3 hours or up to 2 days.

4 Run a thin knife around the edge of the mold to help loosen the gelatin, then dip the mold into a bowl of hot water for about 5 seconds. Invert the mold onto a large chilled serving plate and serve at once.

PER SERVING (1 cup): 133 Cal, 0 g Fat, 0 g Sat Fat, 0 g Trans Fat, 0 mg Chol, 15 mg Sod, 29 g Carb, 1 g Fib, 4 g Prot, 27 mg Calc. **POINTS** value: **2.**

Good Idea   If you have never made—or eaten—homemade "Jell-O," you are in for a real taste treat, as the fresh fruit flavor is intense and delicious. Homemade fruit gelatin is surprisingly easy to make, and once you prepare it, you are sure to make it again and again.

NECTARINE-BLUEBERRY GELATIN CUPS

Nectarine-Blueberry Gelatin Cups

HANDS-ON PREP 15 MIN   COOK 5 MIN   SERVES 8

1½ cups cool water
½ cup sugar
Pinch salt
½ cup fresh lemon juice
   (about 4 lemons)
2 envelopes unflavored gelatin
3 ripe small nectarines (¾ pound), halved,
   pitted, and chopped
1 pint blueberries

1 Combine the water, sugar, and salt in a medium saucepan and set over high heat. Bring to a boil, stirring until the sugar is dissolved; stir in the lemon juice. Remove the saucepan from the heat. Pour 1 cup of the lemon mixture into a small bowl; sprinkle with the gelatin and let soften, about 5 minutes.

2 Heat the lemon mixture over medium heat just until hot; remove the saucepan from the heat. Add the gelatin mixture; stir until the gelatin is completely dissolved. Pour through a fine-mesh sieve set over a medium bowl.

3 Divide the nectarines and blueberries among eight 6- to 8- ounce custard cups or ramekins. Ladle the gelatin mixture over the fruit, pressing on the fruit so it is submerged. Cover with plastic wrap and refrigerate until thoroughly chilled and set, at least 3 hours or up to 2 days.

4 To unmold, run a thin knife around the edges of the cups to loosen the gelatin, then dip the cups into a bowl of hot water about 5 seconds. Invert the cups onto plates, shaking it gently to help free the gelatin; lift off the cups.

PER SERVING (1 gelatin cup): 90 Cal, 0 g Fat, 0 g Sat Fat, 0 g Trans Fat, 0 mg Chol, 43 mg Sod, 21 g Carb, 1 g Fib, 2 g Prot, 7 mg Calc. *POINTS* value: *2.*

Good Idea   This delectable low-calorie dessert can also be made in a 4½ x 8½-inch loaf pan. Cut into 8 slices for serving.

Oven-Roasted Nectarines and Strawberries

HANDS-ON PREP 15 MIN   COOK 20 MIN   SERVES 4

12 strawberries, hulled
4   ripe small nectarines (about 1 pound), halved
    and pitted
1   tablespoon sugar
1   cup lemon sorbet
6   fresh mint leaves, thinly sliced

1 Preheat the oven to 425°F.

2 Put the strawberries and nectarine halves, cut side up, on a baking sheet. Sprinkle with the sugar and roast until softened, about 20 minutes.

3 Place 2 nectarine halves and 3 strawberries on each of 4 plates. Place a 2-tablespoon scoop of sorbet in each nectarine half and sprinkle with the mint. Serve at once.

PER SERVING (1 dessert): 119 Cal, 0 g Fat, 0 g Sat Fat, 0 g Trans Fat, 0 mg Chol, 5 mg Sod, 30 g Carb, 2 g Fib, 1 g Prot, 12 mg Calc. *POINTS* value: *2.*

Try It   This fruit dessert would also be delicious with scoops of passion fruit or mango sorbet instead of the lemon sorbet. Or drizzle the sorbet with chocolate sauce (1 tablespoon of Dark Chocolate Sauce, page 196, will increase the per-serving *POINTS* value by *1).*

Fresh Peach and Ricotta Bruschetta

HANDS-ON PREP 15 MIN   COOK: NONE   SERVES 4

½   cup part-skim ricotta cheese
1½ teaspoons sugar
⅛   teaspoon cinnamon
1   tablespoon unsalted butter, softened
4   (½-inch-thick) slices country-style bread,
    toasted
2   ripe small peaches, peeled and cut into
    ⅜-inch-thick wedges

1 Put the ricotta in a food processor and process until perfectly smooth, 1–2 minutes. Combine the sugar and cinnamon in a small bowl; set aside.

2 To assemble the bruschetta, spread the butter on one side of each slice of the bread. Sprinkle evenly with the cinnamon sugar and top with the peaches. Dollop one-fourth of the ricotta on top of each bruschetta and serve at once.

PER SERVING (1 bruschetta): 153 Cal, 7 g Fat, 4 g Sat Fat, 0 g Trans Fat, 17 mg Chol, 176 mg Sod, 19 g Carb, 2 g Fib, 6 g Prot, 106 mg Calc. **POINTS** value: **3.**

Good Idea   Feel free to use other fresh ripe fruit instead of the peaches; nectarines, plums, cherries, and/or apricots would all be terrific. We like the flavor of a plain country-style bread here, but you can also use a light sourdough, whole-grain bread, or a cranberry-nut bread.

Caramelized Pear Crêpes

HANDS-ON PREP 30 MIN   COOK 30 MIN   SERVES 4

½ cup all-purpose flour

Pinch salt

¾ cup low-fat (1%) milk

¼ cup fat-free egg substitute

1   teaspoon grated orange zest

FILLING

3   firm-ripe pears, such as Anjou, peeled, halved,

cored, and finely chopped

3   tablespoons packed dark brown sugar

2   teaspoons fresh lemon juice

3   teaspoons unsalted butter

1 To make the crêpes, combine the flour and salt in a medium bowl. Whisk together the milk, egg substitute, and orange zest in a small bowl. Gradually whisk the milk mixture into the flour mixture; let rest 15 minutes.

2 Spray a crêpe pan or small (6-inch) nonstick skillet with nonstick spray and set over medium heat until a drop of water sizzles in it. Stir the batter; pour a scant 2 tablespoonfuls of the batter into the center of the skillet, tilting the pan to coat the bottom with the batter. Cook until the top is set and the underside is golden, 1–2 minutes. Turn and cook until golden brown, about 15 seconds. Transfer the crêpe to a plate. Lightly spray the skillet and repeat with remaining batter to make 12 crêpes in all, spraying the pan before adding more batter.

3 Spray a large nonstick skillet with nonstick spray and set over medium-high heat. Add the pears, brown sugar, and lemon juice; cook, stirring, until the pears soften and most of the liquid is evaporated, about 5 minutes. Transfer to a plate and let cool. Lay the crêpes on a work surface and place a generous tablespoonful of the pear mixture in the middle of each crêpe; fold into quarters.

4 Meanwhile, melt 1 teaspoon of the butter in a clean large nonstick skillet set over medium-high heat. Place 4 folded crêpes in the skillet in a single layer and cook until golden brown and crisp, 1–2 minutes. Turn the crêpes and cook until golden brown and crisp, 1–2 minutes. Place the crêpes on a heatproof platter in a single layer; keep warm. Repeat with the remaining butter and crêpes to make 12 crêpes in all. Serve at once.

PER SERVING (3 filled crêpes): 221 Cal, 4 g Fat, 2 g Sat Fat, 0 g Trans Fat, 10 mg Chol, 126 mg Sod, 44 g Carb, 5 g Fib, 5 g Prot, 84 mg Calc. *POINTS* value: *4.*

Tarragon-Poached Pears

HANDS-ON PREP 15 MIN **COOK** 45 MIN **SERVES** 8

4 cups water
1 cup dry white wine or white grape juice
1 cup sugar
1 bunch fresh tarragon
8 (3-inch-long) strips lemon zest, removed with
   a vegetable peeler
1 tablespoon fresh lemon juice
Pinch salt
4 large firm-ripe Bartlett or Bosc pears

1 Combine the water, wine, sugar, all but 8 tiny sprigs of the tarragon, the lemon zest and juice, and salt in a large saucepan and set over high heat. Bring to a boil; boil 10 minutes. Remove the saucepan from the heat.

2 Meanwhile, peel the pears, cut lengthwise in half, and remove the cores with a melon baller or a small knife. Add the pears to the saucepan and set over low heat. Simmer, covered, over low heat until the pears are tender when pierced with a fork, 10–15 minutes. With a slotted spoon, transfer the pears to a large shallow bowl.

3 Bring the poaching liquid to a boil over high heat; boil until reduced to about 2 cups, about 15 minutes. Pour through a fine-mesh sieve set over a small bowl; reserve the zest. Pour the poaching liquid over the pears; add the lemon zest. Cool the pears slightly and serve, or refrigerate, covered, turning occasionally, until thoroughly chilled, at least 3 hours or up to 2 days.

4 Place a pear half in each of 8 shallow bowls and top with some of the syrup; garnish with the remaining tarragon sprigs and the lemon zest.

PER SERVING (½ pear and ¼ cup syrup): 166 Cal, 0 g Fat, 0 g Sat Fat, 0 g Trans Fat, 0 mg Chol, 41 mg Sod, 42 g Carb, 3 g Fib, 0 g Prot, 17 mg Calc. *POINTS* value: **3.**

How We Did It When removing strips of lemon zest, be sure to peel off only the flavorful, colorful yellow part of the zest and not the bitter white pith that is underneath. If the lemon strips do contain bits of pith, use a small, sharp knife to cut it away.

Plum and Toasted Almond Dessert Pizza

HANDS-ON PREP 35 MIN   COOK 1 HR   SERVES 8

DOUGH

1⅓ cups all-purpose flour

½ cup sugar

1 tablespoon baking powder

Pinch salt

⅓ cup part-skim ricotta cheese

2 tablespoons cold unsalted butter, cut into pieces

1 egg white

2 teaspoons low-fat (1%) milk

1¼ teaspoons vanilla extract

TOPPING

1 egg white, lightly beaten

8 ripe purple plums (about 2 pounds), halved, pitted, and thickly sliced

2 tablespoons sugar

2 tablespoons sliced unblanched almonds

1 To make the dough, put the flour, sugar, baking powder, and salt in a food processor; pulse to blend. Add the ricotta, butter, egg white, milk, and vanilla; pulse just until the dough begins to form a ball. Wrap in plastic wrap and refrigerate at least 1 hour or up to overnight.

2 Meanwhile, preheat the oven to 350°F. Lightly spray a large baking sheet with nonstick spray.

3 Roll out the dough between 2 sheets of wax paper to form a 10-inch round. Remove the top sheet of wax paper and flip the dough onto the baking sheet; remove the wax paper. Fold the edge of the dough over to form a ½-inch rim. Bake for 10 minutes. Let cool about 5 minutes on the baking sheet on a rack.

4 Brush the crust with the egg white. Beginning at the edge, arrange the plum slices in concentric circles, overlapping the slices slightly; sprinkle evenly with the sugar. Bake for 40 minutes. Sprinkle the almonds over the fruit and bake until the crust is golden brown and the plums soften but still hold their shape, about 10 minutes longer. Cut into 8 wedges and serve at once.

PER SERVING (1 wedge): 241 Cal, 5 g Fat, 2 g Sat Fat, 0 g Trans Fat, 11 mg Chol, 246 mg Sod, 45 g Carb, 2 g Fib, 5 g Prot, 145 mg Calc. **POINTS** value: **5.**

How We Did It   The dough for the pizza crust is refrigerated before being rolled out for two reasons: to relax the gluten in the flour and to make the dough easier to work with.

PLUM AND TOASTED
ALMOND DESSERT PIZZA

Baked Rhubarb with Raspberries

HANDS-ON PREP 25 MIN   **COOK** 30 MIN   **SERVES** 6

1   (6-ounce) container raspberries
¾   cup packed light brown sugar
¼   cup boiling water
1   pound fresh rhubarb, trimmed and cut into
    ½-inch-thick slices or frozen sliced rhubarb
¼   teaspoon vanilla extract
Pinch salt
6   (⅜-inch-thick) slices thawed frozen
    reduced-fat pound cake

1 Preheat the oven to 350°F.

2 Put the raspberries, brown sugar, and water in a food processor; pulse just until the berries break up. Pour the mixture through a sieve set over a medium bowl, pressing hard on the solids to extract as much liquid as possible; discard the solids. Stir in the rhubarb, vanilla, and salt.

3 Transfer the mixture to a 7 x 11-inch baking dish. Bake until the rhubarb is tender, about 30 minutes, stirring very gently halfway through the baking. Place the baking dish on a rack and cool 10 minutes.

4 Meanwhile, toast the pound cake until golden brown. Place 1 slice of cake on each of 6 plates and top evenly with the rhubarb. Serve at once.

PER SERVING (1 slice cake and ⅔ cup rhubarb): 229 Cal, 5 g Fat, 1 g Sat Fat, 1 g Trans Fat, 21 mg Chol, 148 mg Sod, 46 g Carb, 2 g Fib, 3 g Prot, 196 mg Calc. **POINTS** value: **5.**

Food Note   Rhubarb is more pleasant to eat when its shape is retained, and baking is the best way to ensure this. Feel free to add a little minced crystallized ginger to the rhubarb while it bakes, or add a sprinkle of rosewater (available in specialty food stores) after it is cooked for an exotic touch.

Strawberry-Almond Napoleons

HANDS-ON PREP 25 MIN   COOK 10 MIN   SERVES 8

- **4** (12 x 17-inch) sheets frozen phyllo, thawed
- **8** teaspoons unsalted butter, melted
- **16** teaspoons sugar
- **1½** cups thawed frozen fat-free whipped topping
- **24** small strawberries, hulled and sliced
- **⅓** cup sliced almonds

1 Preheat the oven to 375°F. Lightly spray 2 baking sheets with nonstick spray.

2 Place 1 phyllo sheet on a work surface. Brush with 2 teaspoons of the butter and sprinkle with about 4 teaspoons sugar. Keep the remaining phyllo covered with a damp paper towel and plastic wrap to keep it from drying out. Repeat the layering 3 more times with the remaining phyllo, butter, and sugar. Trim the phyllo stack to make a 12 x 16-inch rectangle. Cut lengwise into 3 strips, then cut crosswire to make twelve 4-inch squares. Cut each square in half on the diagonal to make 24 triangles in all.

3 Place the phyllo triangles on the baking sheets in a single layer. Bake until golden brown, about 10 minutes. Let cool completely on the baking sheets on racks.

4 Top each of 8 phyllo triangles with 1 tablespoon whipped topping, 1 sliced strawberry, and a few sliced almonds. Top each with another triangle so the points are slightly offset from the first triangle. Top each with 1 tablespoon whipped topping, 1 strawberry, and a few sliced almonds. Repeat to make 1 more layer. Place a napoleon on each of 8 plates. Serve at once.

PER SERVING (1 napoleon): 160 Cal, 7 g Fat, 3 g Sat Fat, 0 g Trans Fat, 11 mg Chol, 47 mg Sod, 24 g Carb, 1 g Fib, 2 g Prot, 17 mg Calc. **POINTS** value: **4.**

Good Idea   The unfilled baked phyllo triangles can be stored in an airtight container at room temperature up to 1 day.

STRAWBERRIES WITH
STRAWBERRY-ORANGE SABAYON AND
ALMOND-CITRUS TUILES, PAGE 77

Strawberries with Strawberry-Orange Sabayon

HANDS-ON PREP 20 MIN   COOK 20 MIN   SERVES 4

2   **(1-pound) containers strawberries, hulled**
½   **cup dry white wine or white grape juice**
½   **cup fresh orange juice**
⅓   **cup sugar**
1   **(3-inch-long) strip orange zest, removed with
a vegetable peeler**
3   **egg yolks**

1 Chop enough strawberries to equal 1 cup; set aside. Quarter the remaining strawberries and divide evenly among 4 wineglasses or goblets; set aside.

2 Combine the chopped strawberries, wine, orange juice, sugar, and orange zest in a medium saucepan and set over medium-high heat. Bring to a boil, stirring until the sugar is dissolved. Reduce the heat and simmer until the strawberries are very soft, about 5 minutes. Pour through a fine-mesh sieve set over a small bowl, pressing hard on the solids to extract as much liquid as possible; discard the solids.

3 Meanwhile, fill a medium saucepan with 1½ inches of water and bring almost to a simmer over medium heat. With a hand mixer on medium-high speed, beat the egg yolks in a deep bowl until frothy, about 1 minute. Slowly beat in the warm strawberry mixture. Set the bowl over the saucepan and beat until the mixture is tripled in volume and very thick, about 10 minutes. Remove the bowl from the saucepan. Spoon the sabayon over the strawberries, dividing it evenly. Serve at once.

PER SERVING (1¼ cups sabayon and 1 cup strawberries): 192 Cal, 4 g Fat, 1 g Sat Fat, 0 g Trans Fat, 154 mg Chol, 10 mg Sod, 37 g Carb, 4 g Fib, 4 g Prot, 55 mg Calc. **POINTS** value: **3.**

How We Did It   The lovely foamy pink sauce for the strawberries is wonderful, but make certain you use a deep bowl—the deepest you have—otherwise the sabayon will fly out of the bowl when beaten.

Strawberry-Orange Trifle

HANDS-ON PREP 30 MIN   COOK NONE   SERVES 6

4   (½-inch-thick) slices angel food cake, cut into
½-inch cubes
1   (1-pound) container strawberries
2   tablespoons orange-flavored liqueur or fresh
     orange juice
2   tablespoons sugar
2   cups Custard Sauce (page 201)
2   tablespoons sliced unblanched
     almonds, toasted

1 Place the cake cubes in a footed medium bowl. Reserve 6 strawberries for garnish; hull and slice the remaining berries.

2 Combine the sliced strawberries, liqueur, and sugar in a medium bowl; spoon on top of the cake, then cover with the custard. Refrigerate, covered, until thoroughly chilled, at least 4 hours or up to 8 hours.

3 Divide the trifle evenly among 6 dessert dishes. Sprinkle with the almonds and garnish each serving with a whole strawberry. Serve at once.

PER SERVING (1 generous cup trifle and 1 strawberry): 185 Cal, 2 g Fat, 0 g Sat Fat, 0 g Trans Fat, 2 mg Chol, 263 mg Sod, 36 g Carb, 2 g Fib, 5 g Prot, 63 mg Calc. *POINTS* value: *3.*

Good Idea   If you prefer, you can use reduced-fat pound cake or crumbled meringue instead of the angel food cake. The angel food cake slices can also be toasted (or grilled) before being cubed. For a tasty variation, try fresh raspberries or blackberries; just be sure you use a total of 3 cups fruit.

Mixed Fruit Compote with Bay Leaf and Lemon

HANDS-ON PREP 10 MIN   COOK 10 MIN   SERVES 4

1½ cups apple cider or apple juice

4   small imported bay leaves or 2 California bay leaves, halved

4   (2½-inch-long) strips lemon zest, removed with a vegetable peeler

2   tablespoons packed light brown sugar

Pinch salt

1   (6-ounce) package mixed dried fruit

¼   cup fat-free sour cream or Greek-style yogurt (optional)

1 Combine the apple cider, bay leaves, lemon zest, brown sugar, and salt in a medium saucepan and set over medium-high heat. Bring to a boil, stirring until the sugar is dissolved. Reduce the heat and simmer 2 minutes.

2 Add the dried fruit and bring to a boil. Simmer, covered, stirring occasionally, until the fruit is softened, about 5 minutes. Serve warm or refrigerate, covered, until thoroughly chilled, about 3 hours. Discard the bay leaves. Divide the compote evenly among 4 dessert dishes and top with a dollop of sour cream (if using).

PER SERVING (½ cup compote without sour cream): 174 Cal, 0 g Fat, 0 g Sat Fat, 0 g Trans Fat, 0 mg Chol, 83 mg Sod, 45 g Carb, 3 g Fib, 1 g Prot, 30 mg Calc. **POINTS** value: **3.**

Try It   Instead of the mixed dried fruit, the compote can also be prepared with a 6-ounce package of dried apricots. You'll be happiest if you choose the more flavorful dried apricot halves from California with their dark orange color rather than small whole Turkish apricots.

Creamy Desserts

Chapter 6

MANGO AND COCONUT RICE
PUDDING PARFAITS

Mango and Coconut Rice Pudding Parfaits

HANDS-ON PREP 30 MIN   COOK 1 HR   SERVES 8

2½ cups water

Pinch salt

1 cup long-grain white rice, preferably jasmine or basmati

2 cups low-fat (1%) milk

1 (14-ounce) can light (reduced-fat) coconut milk

¼ cup packed light brown sugar

¼ cup granulated sugar

14 fresh basil leaves

2 firm-ripe mangoes, peeled, pitted, and finely chopped

2 tablespoons fresh lime juice

1 Bring the water and salt to a boil in a heavy medium saucepan set over high heat. Add the rice and reduce the heat to low. Cook, covered, 20 minutes. Remove the saucepan from the heat and let stand, covered, about 10 minutes.

2 Stir the milk, coconut milk, brown sugar, and granulated sugar into the rice and set over medium heat; bring just to a boil. Reduce the heat to low and simmer, stirring frequently, until the mixture is thick and creamy and the rice is very soft, about 30 minutes, stirring constantly during the last 5 minutes of cooking.

3 Spoon the rice pudding into a medium bowl and let cool to room temperature, stirring occasionally. Refrigerate, covered, until chilled, at least 4 hours or up to overnight.

4 Very thinly slice 6 of the basil leaves. Stir together the mango, sliced basil, and lime juice in a small bowl. Spoon ½ cup of the rice pudding into each of 8 glasses. Top each with 2 tablespoons of the mango mixture; cover each with a generous ¼ cup of the rice pudding, then another 2 tablespoons of the mango mixture. Garnish each parfait with a basil leaf and serve at once.

PER SERVING (1 parfait): 234 Cal, 4 g Fat, 3 g Sat Fat, 0 g Trans Fat, 3 mg Chol, 91 mg Sod, 47 g Carb, 2 g Fib, 6 g Prot, 95 mg Calc. **POINTS** value: **5.**

How We Did It To very thinly slice basil leaves like a pro, neatly stack them and roll up lengthwise, jelly-roll style. With a very sharp knife, cut crosswise into the thinnest slices possible.

Rich Chocolate Mousse

HANDS-ON PREP 10 MIN   COOK 2 MIN   SERVES 4

⅔ **cup fat-free half-and-half**

8   **ounces bittersweet or semisweet chocolate,**
      chopped

1   **teaspoon vanilla extract**

Pinch salt

1½ **cups fat-free sour cream**

1 Bring the half-and-half just to a boil in a medium saucepan set over medium heat. Remove the saucepan from the heat and stir in the chocolate. Let stand about 2 minutes, then whisk until the chocolate is melted and the mixture is smooth. Whisk in the vanilla and salt. Transfer to a medium bowl and let cool to room temperature.

2 With an electric mixer on medium-high speed, beat the sour cream in a medium bowl until light and fluffy, about 3 minutes. Reduce the speed to low. Add the chocolate mixture in 3 additions, beating just until combined. Divide the mousse evenly among 4 wineglasses or dessert dishes. Refrigerate, covered, until thoroughly chilled and set, at least 2 hours or up to 1 day.

PER SERVING (¾ cup): 184 Cal, 10 g Fat, 6 g Sat Fat, 0 g Trans Fat, 5 mg Chol, 132 mg Sod, 24 g Carb, 2 g Fib, 4 g Prot, 90 mg Calc. ***POINTS*** value: **4.**

Try It   Add a teaspoon or two of a favorite liqueur, such as raspberry, orange, or hazelnut to the sour cream while beating it; the liqueur will add another layer of flavor.

Buttermilk Panna Cotta

HANDS-ON PREP 15 MIN   COOK 2 MIN   SERVES 4

1½ teaspoons unflavored gelatin
¾ cup fat-free half-and-half
1   cup low-fat buttermilk
⅓ cup sugar
Pinch salt
¾ teaspoon vanilla extract
½ cup Silky Strawberry Sauce (page 202)

1 Spray four 5-ounce ramekins or 6-ounce custard cups with nonstick spray.

2 Sprinkle the gelatin over ½ cup of the half-and-half in a small bowl. Let stand until the gelatin softens, about 5 minutes.

3 Meanwhile, combine the remaining ¼ cup of half-and-half, the buttermilk, sugar, and salt in a medium saucepan and set over medium heat. Cook, whisking, until the sugar is dissolved, about 2 minutes. Remove the saucepan from the heat and whisk in the gelatin mixture until completely dissolved. Whisk in the vanilla. Pour the custard mixture through a fine-mesh sieve set over a medium bowl. Divide the custard evenly among the ramekins. Refrigerate until thoroughly chilled and set, at least 4 hours or up to 1 day.

4 Run a thin knife around the edges of the ramekins to loosen the custards, then dip the ramekins, one at a time, into a bowl of hot water about 5 seconds. Unmold the custards onto chilled plates and spoon 2 tablespoons strawberry sauce around each.

PER SERVING (½ cup custard and 2 tablespoons sauce): 144 Cal, 1 g Fat, 1 g Sat Fat, 0 g Trans Fat, 5 mg Chol, 224 mg Sod, 30 g Carb, 0 g Fib, 4 g Prot, 121 mg Calc. **POINTS** value: **3.**

Food Note The name of this terrific make-ahead dessert, panna cotta, is Italian for "cooked cream," although it is hardly cooked at all. Originally a specialty of the Piedmonte region of Italy, panna cotta is now enjoyed all over Italy and America. Our more healthful version has all of the lushness of a classic panna cotta but with less fat.

Tapioca Pudding with Dried Cherries

HANDS-ON PREP 15 MIN   COOK 10 MIN   SERVES 4

2½ cups fat-free half-and-half

3 (3-inch-long) strips lemon zest, removed with
   a vegetable peeler

⅛ teaspoon ground allspice

½ cup dried tart cherries, dried cranberries, or
   golden raisins

⅓ cup sugar

3 tablespoons quick-cooking tapioca

⅓ cup fat-free egg substitute

½ teaspoon vanilla extract

1 Combine 2 cups of the half-and-half, the lemon zest, and allspice in a heavy large saucepan; bring to a boil. Remove the saucepan from the heat; let stand, covered, about 10 minutes. With a slotted spoon, remove the zest; discard. Stir in the cherries, sugar, and tapioca; let stand, covered, about 5 minutes.

2 Whisk together the egg substitute and the remaining ½ cup of half-and-half in a small bowl; whisk into the cherry mixture. Cook over medium-low heat, stirring frequently, until thickened and bubbly, about 7 minutes. Stir in the vanilla.

3 Divide the pudding evenly among 4 dessert bowls. Serve warm, or let come to room temperature and refrigerate, covered, until thoroughly chilled and set, at least 2 hours or up to 1 day.

PER SERVING (¾ cup): 242 Cal, 2 g Fat, 1 g Sat Fat, 0 g Trans Fat, 8 mg Chol, 256 mg Sod, 50 g Carb, 2 g Fib, 7 g Prot, 165 mg Calc. *POINTS* value: *5.*

How We Did It   After the egg substitute is whisked in, use a heatproof rubber spatula for the stirring, as it's the best tool for scraping down the side of the pan and keeping the pudding from sticking in the curve between the side and the bottom of the saucepan.

Classic Crème Caramel

HANDS-ON PREP 15 MIN   COOK 55 MIN   SERVES 4

⅓ cup + 3 tablespoons sugar
3 tablespoons water
1 cup fat-free half-and-half
½ cup fat-free egg substitute
¼ teaspoon vanilla extract
Pinch salt

1 Preheat the oven to 325°F.

2 Combine ⅓ cup of the sugar and the water in a heavy medium saucepan and set over medium heat. Cook, stirring, until the sugar is dissolved. Increase the heat to high. Boil, without stirring, brushing down the side of the pan with a pastry brush dipped in cool water and swirling the pan to even out the color, until the caramel is dark amber, about 8 minutes. Immediately pour the caramel into four 5-ounce ramekins or 6-ounce custard cups, dividing it evenly and tilting the ramekins to evenly coat the bottoms and about halfway up the sides. Set aside until the caramel is cool and hard.

3 Meanwhile, bring the half-and-half just to a boil in a medium saucepan set over medium heat. Whisk together the egg substitute, the remaining 3 tablespoons of sugar, the vanilla, and salt in a medium bowl. Whisk ½ cup of the hot half-and-half into the egg mixture, then return the mixture to the saucepan and set over medium-low heat. Cook, stirring, until thickened and smooth, about 2 minutes. Immediately pour the custard through a fine-mesh sieve set over a medium bowl.

4 Divide the custard evenly among the ramekins and place in a 9-inch square baking pan. Put the pan in the oven and add enough boiling water to the pan to come halfway up the sides of the ramekins. Bake until the custards are just set around the edges and still jiggle in the center, 35–40 minutes.

5 Carefully transfer the ramekins to a rack and let cool, then refrigerate, covered, until thoroughly chilled and set, at least 4 hours or up to 1 day. Run a thin knife around the edges of the ramekins to loosen the custards. Unmold onto rimmed plates or dessert dishes to catch all the custard sauce.

PER SERVING (1 custard): 152 Cal, 1 g Fat, 1 g Sat Fat, 0 g Trans Fat, 3 mg Chol, 216 mg Sod, 32 g Carb, 0 g Fib, 5 g Prot, 69 mg Calc. *POINTS* value: *3.*

Luscious Butterscotch Pudding

HANDS-ON PREP 10 MIN   COOK 12 MIN   SERVES 6

- ⅔ cup packed dark brown sugar
- 2 tablespoons cornstarch
- 2 cups fat-free half-and-half
- 3 egg yolks
- ¼ teaspoon salt
- 1 teaspoon vanilla extract
- Thawed frozen fat-free whipped topping (optional)
- 2 tablespoons coarsely crushed hard butterscotch candies (optional)

1 Whisk together the brown sugar and cornstarch in a medium saucepan. Slowly whisk in the half-and-half until smooth; set over medium heat. Cook, whisking, until the mixture thickens and bubbles, 8–10 minutes. Remove the saucepan from the heat.

2 Whisk together the egg yolks and salt in a medium bowl. Whisk about ½ cup of the hot half-and-half mixture into the egg mixture. Return the mixture to the saucepan and cook, stirring, over low heat until thickened and bubbly, 1–2 minutes.

3 Pour the pudding through a sieve set over a medium bowl; whisk in the vanilla. Divide the pudding evenly among 6 parfait glasses or dessert dishes and let cool to room temperature. Refrigerate, covered, until thoroughly chilled and set, at least 2 hours or up to 1 day. Served topped with whipped topping and butterscotch candies (if using).

PER SERVING (½ cup without whipped topping and candy): 179 Cal, 3 g Fat, 1 g Sat Fat, 0 g Trans Fat, 106 mg Chol, 228 mg Sod, 34 g Carb, 0 g Fib, 3 g Prot, 109 mg Calc. **POINTS** value: **4.**

Try It   Replace 1 tablespoon of the half-and-half with an equal amount of bourbon or brandy for a more sophisticated pudding, which would be especially appealing during the holiday season.

LUSCIOUS BUTTERSCOTCH
PUDDING

Mocha Pots de Crème

HANDS-ON PREP 15 MIN   COOK 25 MIN   SERVES 4

1   cup fat-free half-and-half
4   ounces bittersweet or semisweet chocolate,
    finely chopped
1   teaspoon instant espresso powder
½   teaspoon vanilla extract
½   cup fat-free egg substitute
¼   cup packed dark brown sugar
Pinch salt
4   whole coffee beans, for garnish (optional)

1 Preheat the oven to 325°F.

2 Bring the half-and-half just to a boil in a medium saucepan set over medium-high heat. Remove the saucepan from the heat. Add the chocolate, espresso powder, and vanilla; whisk until the chocolate is melted and the mixture is smooth.

3 Whisk together the egg substitute, brown sugar, and salt in a medium bowl. Whisk in ½ cup of the half-and-half mixture. Add the remaining half-and-half mixture in a slow, steady stream, whisking constantly. Pour through a fine-mesh sieve set over a medium bowl.

4 Divide the custard evenly among four 5-ounce ramekins or 6-ounce custard cups and place in a 9-inch square baking pan. Put the pan in the oven and add enough boiling water to the pan to come halfway up the sides of the ramekins. Loosely cover the pan with foil to prevent a skin from forming on the custards. Bake until the custards are barely set around the edges and jiggle in the center, about 25 minutes. Do not overbake; the custards will continue to firm up as they cool.

5 Carefully transfer the ramekins to a rack and cool. Refrigerate, covered, until thoroughly chilled and set, at least 3 hours or up to 1 day. Garnish each pots de crème with a coffee bean (if using).

PER SERVING (½ cup custard): 243 Cal, 11 g Fat, 7 g Sat Fat, 0 g Trans Fat, 3 mg Chol, 225 mg Sod, 35 g Carb, 3 g Fib, 7 g Prot, 94 mg Calc. *POINTS* value: **5.**

Food Note   Pots de crème (POH-duh-crehm), French for "pots of cream," is the term for both the custard and the decorative small lidded pots they are often baked in. The classic flavor for pots de crème is vanilla, but renditions for coffee, chocolate, maple, and even pumpkin are equally popular.

Coeur à la Crème

HANDS-ON PREP 15 MIN   COOK NONE   SERVES 4

1 (8-ounce) package fat-free cream cheese

1 cup fat-free sour cream

¼ cup confectioners' sugar

1 teaspoon fresh lemon juice

½ teaspoon vanilla extract

Pinch salt

½ cup Fresh Raspberry-Orange Sauce (page 204)

1 cup mixed berries

1 With an electric mixer on medium speed, beat the cream cheese, sour cream, confectioners' sugar, lemon juice, vanilla, and salt in a medium bowl until very smooth, about 4 minutes, scraping down the bowl once or twice. Press the mixture though a fine-mesh sieve set over a medium bowl.

2 Cut four 6 x 8-inch pieces of cheesecloth. Rinse under cold water and wring dry. Line four 3-inch heart-shaped coeur à la crème molds with the cheesecloth, letting it drape over the sides of the molds. Divide the cheese mixture evenly among the molds and smooth the tops. Fold the cheesecloth over the cheese mixture, pressing down lightly. Place the molds in a shallow baking dish to catch any drips and refrigerate at least 4 hours or up to 2 days.

3 Unfold the cheesecloth and invert the coeurs onto plates; remove the molds and cheesecloth. Let stand at room temperature 10 minutes. Spoon the sauce around each coeur and garnish with the berries. Serve at once.

PER SERVING (1 coeur, 2 tablespoons sauce, and ¼ cup berries): 166 Cal, 1 g Fat, 1 g Sat Fat, 0 g Trans Fat, 10 mg Chol, 465 mg Sod, 29 g Carb, 3 g Fib, 11 g Prot, 193 mg Calc. **POINTS** value: *3.*

Good Idea If you don't have coeur à la crème molds, trim four 12-ounce paper cups so they are 3 inches high. With a small bamboo skewer, poke about 10 holes in the bottom of each cup. Line the cups with the dampened cheesecloth and proceed as directed in the recipe.

Cherry-Pistachio Cannoli Cream

HANDS-ON PREP 15 MIN   COOK NONE   SERVES 4

1   cup part-skim ricotta cheese
2   tablespoons packed light brown sugar
Pinch salt
¼   cup mini semisweet chocolate chips
¼   teaspoon grated orange zest
¼   teaspoon vanilla extract
2   cups sweet cherries, such as Bing, pitted,
    plus 4 cherries on the stem
2   tablespoons chopped pistachios

1 Combine the ricotta, brown sugar, and salt in a food processor; process until perfectly smooth, 1–2 minutes.

2 Scrape the cheese mixture into a medium bowl; stir in the chocolate chips, orange zest, and vanilla. Refrigerate until thoroughly chilled, at least 1 hour or up to 3 hours.

3 Stir the pitted cherries into the cheese mixture. Divide the cannoli cream evenly among 4 dessert bowls. Sprinkle with the pistachios and top each with a cherry on the stem. Serve at once.

PER SERVING (generous ½ cup): 155 Cal, 7 g Fat, 3 g Sat Fat, 0 g Trans Fat, 13 mg Chol, 101 mg Sod, 20 g Carb, 2 g Fib, 6 g Prot, 127 mg Calc. **POINTS** value: **3.**

Try It   In Sicily, cannoli cream is most often made with fresh sheep's milk ricotta. Now that sheep's milk cheeses are available at greenmarkets and in specialty food markets, you might want to give it a try. Sheep's milk will give the cannoli cream a very tempting flavor, a little bit like a very mild goat cheese—different and temptingly delicious.

Cold Lemon Soufflés

HANDS-ON PREP 50 MIN   COOK NONE   SERVES 8

- 1 envelope unflavored gelatin
- ¼ cup water
- 1½ cups sugar
- ¼ cup grated lemon zest (about 3 large lemons)
- 6 large eggs, separated, at room temperature
- ¾ cup + 2 tablespoons fresh lemon juice
     (about 4 large lemons)
- ¼ teaspoon salt
- 2 cups fat-free sour cream
- Blueberry Sauce (page 203, optional)

1 Wrap a folded strip of heavy-duty foil around each of eight 6-ounce soufflé dishes to form a collar that extends 2 inches above the rims; secure with tape. Spray the insides of the dishes and foil with nonstick spray.

2 Sprinkle the gelatin over the water in a small bowl. Let stand until softened, about 5 minutes. Place the bowl in a larger bowl of hot water and stir until the gelatin is completely dissolved.

3 Put 1 cup of the sugar and the lemon zest in a food processor; pulse until finely ground. With an electric mixer on medium speed, beat the egg yolks, lemon-sugar mixture, lemon juice, and salt in a deep large bowl until combined. Fill a medium saucepan with about 1½ inches of water and bring almost to a simmer over medium-low heat. Set the bowl with the egg yolk mixture over the saucepan and beat until very thick and pale or 160°F on an instant-read thermometer, about 15 minutes. Remove the bowl from the saucepan. Add the gelatin mixture and beat until the mixture comes to room temperature; set aside.

4 With clean beaters and the mixer on medium speed, beat the egg whites in a large bowl until soft peaks form. Increase the speed to medium-high. Beat in the remaining ½ cup sugar, 1 tablespoon at a time, until stiff.

5 Beat the sour cream on medium-high speed in a medium bowl until fluffy, about 3 minutes. Place the bowl containing the egg yolk mixture in a larger bowl filled with ice water and whisk just until the mixture begins to thicken. Gently fold in the sour cream, then the beaten egg whites just until no white streaks remain. Divide evenly among the soufflé dishes; smooth the tops. Refrigerate until chilled and set, at least 3 hours or up to overnight. Remove the collars and serve at once with blueberry sauce (if using).

PER SERVING (1 soufflé without blueberry sauce): 258 Cal, 4 g Fat, 1 g Sat Fat, 0 g Trans Fat, 164 mg Chol, 212 mg Sod, 49 g Carb, 0 g Fib, 7 g Prot, 102 mg Calc. **POINTS** value: **5.**

Baked Bittersweet Chocolate Soufflé

HANDS-ON PREP 25 MIN   COOK 40 MIN   SERVES 12

1   tablespoon + ¼ cup sugar
7   ounces bittersweet or semisweet chocolate, chopped
1   cup fat-free egg substitute
2   tablespoons unsalted butter, softened
5   egg whites
Pinch salt
2   cups Dark Chocolate Sauce (page 198, optional)

1 Place a rack in the middle of the oven and preheat the oven to 425°F. Spray a 1½-quart soufflé dish with nonstick spray and dust with 1 tablespoon of the sugar, shaking out the excess.

2 Fill a medium saucepan with 1½ inches of water and set over medium-low heat; bring almost to a simmer. Put the chocolate in a medium bowl and set over the water; whisk until the chocolate is melted and smooth. Remove the bowl from the saucepan and whisk in the egg substitute and butter until blended; set aside.

3 With an electric mixer on medium-high speed, beat the egg whites and salt in a large bowl until soft peaks form. Add the remaining ¼ cup of sugar, 1 tablespoon at a time, beating until stiff, glossy peaks form.

4 Whisk one-fourth of the beaten whites into the chocolate mixture to lighten it. With a rubber spatula, gently fold in the remaining whites just until no streaks of white remain. Gently pour the mixture into the soufflé dish and smooth the top. Put the soufflé dish in a 9 x 13-inch baking pan. Put in the oven and add enough boiling water to the pan to reach 1 inch up the side of the soufflé dish. Bake until the soufflé is set but the center still jiggles, about 40 minutes. Serve at once with the chocolate sauce.

PER SERVING (¾ cup soufflé and about 2½ tablespoons chocolate sauce): 223 Cal, 14 g Fat, 9 g Sat Fat, 0 g Trans Fat, 5 mg Chol, 113 mg Sod, 25 g Carb, 3 g Fib, 6 g Prot, 27 mg Calc. **POINTS** value: **5.**

How We Did It Grating chocolate is often a messy affair, with the chocolate scattering everywhere. We like to grate chocolate by placing a pie plate in the sink and setting a box grater in it. Then if the chocolate scatters it remains in the sink, which makes for easy cleanup. Move the faucet out of the way so there is no chance of water getting into the chocolate.

BAKED BITTERSWEET
CHOCOLATE SOUFFLÉ AND
CHOCOLATE-DIPPED
MERINGUE FINGERS, PAGE 84

Peach-Blueberry Clafouti

HANDS-ON PREP 20 MIN   COOK 40 MIN   SERVES 8

- 1   cup fat-free half-and-half
- ½   cup fat-free egg substitute
- 1   cup cake flour
- ⅓   cup granulated sugar
- ½   teaspoon vanilla extract
- Pinch salt
- 1   ripe peach, peeled, halved, pitted, and chopped
- ¾   cup blueberries
- 1   tablespoon confectioners' sugar

1 Bring the half-and-half to a boil in a medium saucepan set over medium-high heat. Remove the saucepan from the heat; set aside.

2 Put the egg substitute in a medium bowl. Gradually whisk in the flour, then the granulated sugar, vanilla, and salt until blended. Whisk in the hot half-and-half (the batter will be lumpy); set aside for 1 hour.

3 Meanwhile, preheat the oven to 400°F. Spray a 9-inch round cake pan with nonstick spray.

4 Stir the batter well and pour into the pan. Dot the surface evenly with the peach and blueberries. Bake until puffed and light golden brown, 35–40 minutes. Dust with the confectioners' sugar. Cut into wedges and serve warm.

PER SERVING (⅛ of dessert): 137 Cal, 1 g Fat, 0 g Sat Fat, 0 g Trans Fat, 2 mg Chol, 108 mg Sod, 29 g Carb, 1 g Fib, 4 g Prot, 38 mg Calc. *POINTS* value: *3.*

Zap It   Use your microwave to bring the half-and-half to a boil: Pour the half-and-half into a 2-quart glass measuring cup or bowl and microwave on High until it begins to boil, which will take about 2 minutes. The generous size of the measuring cup is insurance against the half-and-half boiling over.

Winter-Spiced Pumpkin Bread Pudding

HANDS-ON PREP 30 MIN   COOK 1 HOUR 15 MIN   SERVES 12

- 3 cups fat-free half-and-half
- 1 cup fat-free egg substitute
- ½ cup packed dark brown sugar
- ¾ teaspoon pumpkin pie spice
- ¼ teaspoon salt
- 1 cup canned pumpkin puree
- ½ cup golden raisins
- ¾ teaspoon vanilla extract
- 1 (1-pound) loaf day-old whole-wheat bread, cut into 1½-inch squares
- ½ cup chopped walnuts

1 Bring the half-and-half to a boil in a medium saucepan set over medium-high heat. Remove the saucepan from the heat. Whisk together the egg substitute, brown sugar, pumpkin pie spice, and salt in a medium bowl. Slowly add ½ cup of the hot half-and-half, whisking constantly. Return the mixture to the saucepan and set over medium-low heat. Cook, whisking constantly, until the custard thickens and coats the back of a spoon, about 5 minutes. Immediately pour the custard through a fine-mesh sieve set over a medium bowl.

2 Whisk in the pumpkin, raisins, and vanilla. Add the bread, gently stirring until moistened. Let stand at room temperature about 20 minutes.

3 Meanwhile, preheat the oven to 325°F. Spray a 10-cup baking dish or casserole with nonstick spray.

4 Pour the pudding mixture into the baking dish and spread evenly; sprinkle with the walnuts. Cover the baking dish tightly with foil and place in a roasting pan. Add enough boiling water to the roasting pan to come halfway up the sides of the baking dish. Bake for 1 hour. Uncover and bake until a knife inserted into the center comes out clean, about 15 minutes longer.

5 Carefully lift out the bread pudding and transfer to a rack. Let cool about 20 minutes to serve warm, or serve at room temperature.

PER SERVING (¹⁄₁₂ of bread pudding): 239 Cal, 5 g Fat, 1 g Sat Fat, 0 g Trans Fat, 3 mg Chol, 438 mg Sod, 41 g Carb, 2 g Fib, 8 g Prot, 143 mg Calc. *POINTS* value: *5.*

How We Did It   The key to a silky smooth custard is gentle heat, which is accomplished by baking the bread pudding in a hot water bath. It ensures that the custard will be baked at a constant, gentle low heat throughout the baking time.

VERY LEMONY PUDDING CAKES

Very Lemony Pudding Cakes

HANDS-ON PREP 30 MIN   COOK 30 MIN   SERVES 8

3 tablespoons unsalted butter, softened
1 cup granulated sugar
2 tablespoons grated lemon zest
½ cup fat-free egg substitute
1 cup fat-free sour cream
⅓ cup fresh lemon juice (about 3 lemons)
⅓ cup all-purpose flour
3 egg whites
¼ teaspoon salt
1 tablespoon confectioners' sugar
Lemon curls (optional)

1 Preheat the oven to 350°F. Spray eight 5-ounce ramekins or 6-ounce custard cups with nonstick spray.

2 With an electric mixer on medium speed, beat the butter in a medium bowl until creamy, about 2 minutes. Add the granulated sugar and lemon zest and beat until light and fluffy, about 1 minute. Beat in the egg substitute; reduce the speed to low. Add ½ cup of the sour cream, 3 tablespoons of the lemon juice, and 3 tablespoons of the flour, beating just until smooth. Add the remaining ½ cup of sour cream and the remaining lemon juice and flour; beat until smooth. Set aside.

3 With clean beaters and the mixer on medium speed, beat the egg whites and salt in a medium bowl just until stiff peaks form. With a rubber spatula, fold the beaten whites, one-half at a time, into the lemon mixture, just until no streaks of white remain.

4 Divide the mixture among the ramekins; place in a 9 x 13-inch baking pan. Put the pan in the oven and add enough boiling water to the pan to come 1 inch up the sides of the ramekins. Bake until golden brown and the just set in the center, about 30 minutes. Carefully transfer the ramekins to a rack and let cool about 10 minutes.

5 Dust the tops of the pudding cakes with the confectioners' sugar. Garnish each serving with lemon curls (if using). Serve warm.

PER SERVING (¾ cup): 197 Cal, 4 g Fat, 3 g Sat Fat, 0 g Trans Fat, 14 mg Chol, 169 mg Sod, 36 g Carb, 0 g Fib, 5 g Prot, 49 mg Calc. **POINTS** value: **4.**

Chocolate Truffles

HANDS-ON PREP 20 MIN   COOK 5 MIN   SERVES 32

8   ounces bittersweet or semisweet chocolate,
    chopped
3   tablespoons unsalted butter
⅓   cup fat-free half-and-half
3   tablespoons finely chopped toasted hazelnuts
3   tablespoons unsweetened cocoa powder

1 Line a 5 x 9-inch loaf pan with plastic wrap; spray with nonstick spray.

2 Combine the chocolate and butter in a medium saucepan and set over low heat. Cook, stirring often, until melted and smooth. Remove the saucepan from the heat and stir in the half-and-half until well blended.

3 Scrape the chocolate mixture into the loaf pan and spread evenly. Cover tightly with plastic wrap and refrigerate until firm, at least 3 hours or up to 2 days.

4 Put the hazelnuts and cocoa powder on 2 separate plates. Invert the loaf pan onto a cutting board; remove the plastic wrap. With a sharp knife, cut the chocolate mixture into 32 equal squares. Lightly coat half of the squares in the hazelnuts and half in the cocoa powder. Place the truffles in a covered container, separating the layers with sheets of wax paper. Refrigerate up to 1 week.

PER SERVING (1 truffle): 53 Cal, 4 g Fat, 2 g Sat Fat, 0 g Trans Fat, 3 mg Chol, 5 mg Sod, 4 g Carb, 1 g Fib, 1 g Prot, 7 mg Calc. **POINTS** value: *1.*

HOW WE DID IT   We find it easier—and neater—to cut the chilled truffle mixture into squares rather than rolling it into balls.

Frozen Desserts

Chapter 7

Blueberry-Ginger Sorbet

HANDS-ON PREP 15 MIN   COOK 8 MIN   SERVES 8

2   **cups water**
½   **cup packed light brown sugar**
2   **(3-inch-long) strips lemon zest, removed with**
     a vegetable peeler
2   **tablespoon minced peeled fresh ginger**
Pinch salt
2   **tablespoons fresh lemon juice**
3   **cups fresh or thawed frozen blueberries**
Slivered crystallized ginger (optional)

1 To make the sugar syrup, combine the water, brown sugar, lemon zest, fresh ginger, and salt in a medium saucepan and set over high heat. Bring to a boil, stirring until the sugar is dissolved. Reduce the heat and simmer 5 minutes. Remove the saucepan from the heat and let stand 5 minutes. Pour the syrup through a fine-mesh sieve set over a large bowl; stir in the lemon juice.

2 Put the blueberries and 1 cup of the sugar syrup in a blender or food processor and puree. Stir into the sugar syrup in the bowl. Pour the blueberry mixture through a sieve set over a medium bowl, pressing hard on the solids to extract as much liquid as possible; discard the solids. Cover the blueberry mixture and refrigerate until thoroughly chilled, about 2 hours.

3 Transfer the blueberry mixture to an ice-cream maker and freeze according to the manufacturer's instructions. Transfer the sorbet to a freezer container and freeze until firm, at least 2 hours or up to 6 hours. Serve topped with crystallized ginger (if using). This sorbet is best served the day it's made.

PER SERVING (⅔ cup): 84 Cal, 0 g Fat, 0 g Sat Fat, 0 g Trans Fat, 0 mg Chol, 44 mg Sod, 22 g Carb, 1 g Fib, 43 g Prot, 17 mg Calc. **POINTS** value: **1.**

Food Note Since you might have to purchase a larger piece of ginger than you will need, here is how to store it: Place the ginger in a cool, dry place for up to 3 days or in the crisper drawer of the refrigerator up to 3 weeks, wrapped in a paper towel and placed in a plastic bag. Fresh ginger also freezes well. Peel and cut it into thin slices, then store in a zip-close freezer bag, or freeze the whole peeled piece and cut off slices of the still-frozen ginger as you need it.

BLUEBERRY-GINGER
SORBET

Cantaloupe Sorbet

HANDS-ON PREP 15 MIN   COOK 8 MIN   SERVES 8

½ cup water
½   cup sugar
2   (3-inch-long) strips lime or lemon zest,
    removed with a vegetable peeler
½ teaspoon fennel seeds, lightly crushed
Pinch salt
1   tablespoon fresh lime or lemon juice
1   chilled ripe cantaloupe (3 1/2 pounds), peeled,
halved, seeded, and chopped

1 To make the sugar syrup, combine the water, sugar, lime zest, fennel seeds, and salt in a small saucepan and set over high heat. Bring to a boil, stirring until the sugar is dissolved. Reduce the heat and simmer 5 minutes; stir in the lime juice. Pour the syrup through a sieve set over a small bowl. Cover and refrigerate until thoroughly chilled, about 30 minutes.

2 Meanwhile, puree the cantaloupe in a blender or food processor. Transfer to a medium bowl and whisk in the sugar syrup. Pour the cantaloupe mixture through a sieve set over a large bowl, pressing hard on the solids to extract as much as the liquid as possible; discard the solids.

3 Transfer the cantaloupe mixture to an ice-cream maker and freeze according to the manufacturer's instructions. Transfer the sorbet to a freezer container and freeze until firm, at least 2 hours or up to 6 hours. This sorbet is best served the day it's made.

PER SERVING (½ cup): 83 Cal, 0 g Fat, 0 g Sat Fat, 0 g Trans Fat, 0 mg Chol, 17 mg Sod, 21 g Carb, 1 g Fib, 1 g Prot, 10 mg Calc. **POINTS** value: *1.*

How We Did It Planning ahead and refrigerating the melon until well chilled before making the sorbet really cuts down on the prep time. But if you forget to do it, just allow an extra hour or so for the mixture to chill before it is turned into sorbet.

Chocolate Sorbet

HANDS-ON PREP 20 MIN   COOK 5 MIN   SERVES 8

2½ cups water

¾ cup packed light brown sugar

½ cup granulated sugar

⅔ cup unsweetened cocoa powder

Pinch salt

4 ounces bittersweet or semisweet chocolate, finely chopped

2 teaspoons vanilla extract

1 Combine the water, brown sugar, granulated sugar, cocoa, and salt in a heavy medium saucepan and set over medium-high heat. Bring just to a boil, stirring until the sugar is dissolved. Remove the saucepan from the heat; add the chocolate and whisk until the chocolate is melted and the mixture is smooth. Pour the chocolate mixture through a fine-mesh sieve set over a medium bowl. Let cool to room temperature; stir in the vanilla. Cover and refrigerate until thoroughly chilled, about 3 hours.

2 Transfer the chocolate mixture to an ice-cream maker and freeze according to the manufacturer's instructions. Transfer the sorbet to a freezer container and freeze until firm, at least 2 hours or up to 6 hours. This sorbet is best served the day it's made.

PER SERVING (½ cup): 215 Cal, 6 g Fat, 4 g Sat Fat, 0 g Trans Fat, 0 mg Chol, 49 mg Sod, 44 g Carb, 4 g Fib, 2 g Prot, 36 mg Calc. **POINTS** value: *4.*

Food Note   Bittersweet and semisweet chocolates are interchangeable in most recipes. The amount of chocolate liquor in bittersweet chocolate varies, depending on the brand. It can range from 64 to 70 percent: the more chocolate liquor it contains, the more intense (and bitter) the flavor.

COFFEE GRANITA WITH
WHIPPED TOPPING AND
MINI CHOCOLATE
BROWNIE BISCOTTI, PAGE 86

Coffee Granita with Whipped Topping

HANDS-ON PREP 10 MIN   COOK NONE   SERVES 4

2   **cups hot espresso or very strong brewed**
     coffee
½   **cup packed light brown sugar**
Pinch salt
½   **cup thawed frozen fat-free whipped topping**

1 Combine the espresso, brown sugar, and salt in a medium bowl; stir until the sugar is dissolved. Cool to room temperature, then cover and refrigerate until thoroughly chilled, about 1 hour.

2 Pour the coffee mixture into an 8-inch square baking pan. Cover tightly with foil and freeze until frozen along the edges, about 1 hour. With a fork, scrape the ice at the edges in toward the center. Repeat every 30 minutes, until the granita is semifirm, about 2 hours.

3 Use a fork to scrape across the surface of the granita, transferring the ice shards to 4 glass dishes or wineglasses. Top each serving with 2 tablespoons whipped topping and serve at once.

PER SERVING (¾ cup granita and 2 tablespoons whipped topping): 129 Cal, 2 g Fat, 2 g Sat Fat, 0 g Trans Fat, 0 mg Chol, 99 mg Sod, 29 g Carb, 0 g Fib, 0 g Prot, 28 mg Calc. **POINTS** value: **3.**

Food Note   A cup of espresso equals about ¼ cup of liquid, so you will need to make many cups if you use espresso here. We suggest strong brewed coffee as an alternative, which can be caffeinated or decaffeinated. Or save time and go to your favorite coffee shop and buy the coffee already made.

Pomegranate-Raspberry Granita

HANDS-ON PREP 12 MIN   COOK 4 MIN   SERVES 12

1 **cup water**
⅓ **cup packed light brown sugar**
½ **teaspoon grated lime zest**
Pinch salt
2 **(6-ounce) containers raspberries**
2 **cups pomegranate juice**
3 **tablespoons fresh lime juice**

1 Combine the water, brown sugar, lime zest, and salt in a medium saucepan and set over high heat. Bring to a boil, stirring until the sugar is dissolved. Remove the saucepan from the heat and stir in the raspberries. Puree the raspberry mixture in a food processor. Pour the berry mixture through a sieve set over a large bowl, pressing hard on the solids to extract as much liquid as possible; discard the solids. Stir in the pomegranate juice and lime juice.

2 Pour the fruit mixture into a 9 x 13-inch baking pan. Cover with foil and freeze until frozen along the edges, about 1 hour. With a fork, scrape the ice along the edges in toward the center. Repeat every 30 minutes until the granita is semifirm, about 2 hours.

3 Use a fork to scrape across the surface of the granita, transferring the ice shards to 12 dessert dishes. Serve at once.

PER SERVING (⅔ cup): 51 Cal, 0 g Fat, 0 g Sat Fat, 0 g Trans Fat, 0 mg Chol, 29 mg Sod, 13 g Carb, 1 g Fib, 0 g Prot, 15 mg Calc. **POINTS** value: **1.**

Try It Once hard to find, 100-percent pure pomegranate juice is now available in supermarkets in the juice aisle. This ruby red, flavorful, high-in-antioxidant juice, makes fabulous granita—*and* a delicious drink when mixed with a splash of tonic and a squeeze of fresh lime.

Frozen Vanilla-Bean Yogurt

HANDS-ON PREP 20 MIN   COOK NONE   SERVES 8

½ **vanilla bean**
2 **cups plain low-fat yogurt**
2 **cups fat-free half-and-half**
1 **cup packed light brown sugar**
1 **tablespoon fresh lemon juice**
1 **teaspoon grated lemon zest**
Pinch salt

1 With a small, sharp knife, split the vanilla bean lengthwise in half and scrape out the seeds. Combine the vanilla-bean seeds and the remaining ingredients in a large bowl, whisking until the sugar is dissolved.

2 Pour the yogurt mixture into an ice-cream maker and freeze according to the manufacturer's instructions. Transfer the yogurt to a freezer container and freeze until firm, at least 2 hours or up to 6 hours. This frozen yogurt is best served the day it's made.

PER SERVING (½ cup): 179 Cal, 2 g Fat, 1 g Sat Fat, 0 g Trans Fat, 7 mg Chol, 177 mg Sod, 37 g Carb, 0 g Fib, 5 g Prot, 196 mg Calc. **POINTS** value: **4.**

Good Idea Place small scoops of the frozen yogurt on very thin slices of cantaloupe, or spoon some Fresh Raspberry-Orange Sauce (page 204) around it and sprinkle with some ripe blackberries for a refreshing warm-weather treat.

FROZEN STRAWBERRY YOGURT WITH
DARK CHOCOLATE SAUCE, PAGE 196

Frozen Strawberry Yogurt

HANDS-ON PREP 20 MIN   COOK NONE   SERVES 8

1   (1-pound) container strawberries, hulled
    and chopped
1   cup sugar
2   tablespoons fresh lemon juice
Pinch salt
1   cup vanilla low-fat yogurt
1   cup fat-free half-and-half
Dark chocolate sauce (page 196, optional)

1 Combine the strawberries, sugar, lemon juice, and salt in a medium bowl; let stand, stirring occasionally, about 30 minutes.

2 Meanwhile, whisk together the yogurt and half-and-half in a large bowl; stir in the strawberry mixture. Cover and refrigerate until thoroughly chilled, about 2 hours.

3 Pour the yogurt mixture into an ice-cream maker and freeze according to the manufacturer's instructions. Transfer the yogurt to a freezer container and freeze until firm, at least 2 hours or up to 6 hours. This frozen yogurt is best served the day it's made. Serve with chocolate sauce (if using).

PER SERVING (½ cup without chocolate sauce): 159 Cal, 1 g Fat, 1 g Sat Fat, 0 g Trans Fat, 3 mg Chol, 100 mg Sod, 37 g Carb, 1 g Fib, 3 g Prot, 91 mg Calc. *POINTS* value: *3.*

Express Lane   Rather than chopping the strawberries, here's an even quicker way to prepare them: roughly slice the berries directly into a bowl, then mash with a potato masher.

Raspberry Ice Cream

HANDS-ON PREP 15 MIN   COOK NONE   SERVES 8

2   (6-ounce) containers raspberries
⅔ cup sugar
2   tablespoons fresh lemon juice
1½ cups fat-free half-and-half
1½ cups fat-free sour cream
1   teaspoon rosewater (optional)
Pinch salt

1 Combine the raspberries, sugar, and lemon juice in a food processor; pulse just until the berries are broken up. Pour the berry mixture through a sieve set over a large bowl, pressing hard on the solids to extract as much liquid as possible; discard the solids. Whisk in the half-and-half, sour cream, rosewater (if using) and salt. Cover and refrigerate until thoroughly chilled, about 2 hours.

2 Pour the raspberry mixture into an ice-cream maker and freeze according to the manufacturer's instructions. Transfer the ice cream to a freezer container; freeze until firm, at least 2 hours or up to 6 hours. This ice cream is best served the day it's made.

PER SERVING (½ cup): 142 Cal, 1 g Fat, 0 g Sat Fat, 0 g Trans Fat, 6 mg Chol, 166 mg Sod, 32 g Carb, 2 g Fib, 3 g Prot, 108 mg Calc. **POINTS** value: **3.**

Express Lane Instead of refrigerating the ice-cream mixture before churning it, you can use a quick-chill method to cool it down: Place the ice-cream mixture in a large glass measuring cup and set in a large shallow bowl filled with ice cubes and water. Set aside at cool room temperature or in the refrigerator, stirring occasionally and adding fresh ice as needed, until the ice-cream mixture is cold, about 30 minutes.

Roasted Banana and Pecan Ice Cream

HANDS-ON PREP 25 MIN   COOK 20 MIN   SERVES 12

4   ripe medium bananas, unpeeled

¾   cup coarsely chopped pecans

2   cups fat-free half-and-half

1   cup low-fat (1%) milk

½   cup packed dark brown sugar

2   tablespoons light or dark rum, or orange juice

1   cup fat-free egg substitute

Pinch salt

1½ teaspoons vanilla extract

1 Preheat the oven to 350°F.

2 With the tip of a small knife, pierce each banana 5 times. Put the bananas and pecans on a baking sheet. Roast, tossing the pecans once or twice, until the banana skins are very dark and the pecans are fragrant, about 15 minutes. Let cool on the baking sheet.

3 Meanwhile, combine the half-and-half, milk, brown sugar, and rum in a heavy medium saucepan and set over medium-high heat. Bring just to a boil, stirring until the sugar is dissolved.

4 Whisk together the egg substitute and salt in a medium bowl. Slowly add ½ cup of the hot half-and-half mixture, whisking constantly. Return the mixture to the saucepan and set over medium-low heat. Cook, whisking constantly, until the custard thickens and coats the back of a spoon, about 5 minutes (do not let boil). Remove the saucepan from the heat.

5 When cool enough to handle, make a lengthwise slit in each banana skin and remove the banana; put in a food processor and puree. Whisk the banana puree and vanilla into the custard. Pour the custard mixture through a sieve set over a large bowl, pressing hard on the solids to extract as much liquid as possible. Let cool to room temperature, whisking occasionally. Cover and refrigerate until thoroughly chilled, about 3 hours.

6 Pour the custard mixture into an ice-cream maker and freeze according to the manufacturer's instructions, adding the pecans about 10 minutes before the ice cream is done. Transfer the ice cream to a freezer container and freeze until firm, at least 2 hours or up to 6 hours. This ice cream is best served the day it's made.

PER SERVING (½ cup): 167 Cal, 6 g Fat, 1 g Sat Fat, 0 g Trans Fat, 3 mg Chol, 134 mg Sod, 24 g Carb, 2 g Fib, 5 g Prot, 84 mg Calc. *POINTS* value: *3.*

Fresh Mint–Chocolate Chip Ice Cream

HANDS-ON PREP 20 MIN   COOK 8 MIN   SERVES 10

- 4 **cups fat-free half-and-half**
- 2 **cups packed fresh mint leaves**
- ½ **cup sugar**
- 1 **cup fat-free egg substitute**
- **Pinch salt**
- 1 **cup mini semisweet chocolate chips**

1 Combine the half-and-half, mint, and sugar in a large saucepan and set over medium-high heat. Bring just to a boil, stirring until the sugar is dissolved. Remove the saucepan from the heat; cover and let stand about 10 minutes. Pour the mint mixture through a sieve set over a large bowl, pressing hard on the solids to extract as much liquid as possible; discard the solids.

2 Whisk together the egg substitute and salt in a medium bowl. Slowly add ½ cup of the hot half-and-half mixture, whisking constantly. Return the mixture to saucepan and set over medium-low heat. Cook, whisking slowly and constantly, until the custard thickens and coats the back of a spoon, about 5 minutes (do not let boil).

3 Immediately pour the custard through a fine-mesh sieve set over a large bowl. Let cool to room temperature, whisking occasionally. Cover and refrigerate until thoroughly chilled, about 3 hours.

4 Pour the custard mixture into an ice-cream maker and freeze according to the manufacturer's instructions, adding the chocolate chips about 10 minutes before the ice cream is done. Transfer the ice cream to a freezer container and freeze until firm, at least 2 hours or up to 6 hours. This ice cream is best served the day it's made.

PER SERVING (½ cup): 189 Cal, 6 g Fat, 4 g Sat Fat, 0 g Trans Fat, 5 mg Chol, 216 mg Sod, 30 g Carb, 1 g Fib, 6 g Prot, 107 mg Calc. **POINTS** value: **4.**

How We Did It   You'll need 1 large or 2 small bunches of fresh mint to get 2 cups of packed mint leaves. Briefly rinse the mint sprigs under cold running water; shake off the excess water and gently pat the mint leaves dry with paper towels.

FRESH MINT–CHOCOLATE CHIP
ICE CREAM

Raspberry Creamsicle Cake

HANDS-ON PREP 35 MIN   COOK 25 MIN   SERVES 12

1   cup cake flour
1½ teaspoons baking powder
¼   teaspoon salt
½   cup fat-free egg substitute
¾   cup sugar
¼   cup hot water
2   tablespoons unsalted butter, melted
1   teaspoon vanilla extract
1   quart fat-free vanilla ice cream, slightly
    softened
1   pint raspberry sorbet, slightly softened

1 Preheat the oven to 350°F. Spray a 9-inch square baking pan with nonstick spray. Line with wax paper; spray with nonstick spray.

2 Whisk together the cake flour, baking powder, and salt in a medium bowl; set aside. With an electric mixer on high speed, beat the egg substitute in a large bowl until thickened, about 3 minutes. Gradually add the sugar, beating until fluffy, about 3 minutes. Reduce the speed to low. Beat in the water, melted butter, and vanilla until combined. Add the flour mixture and beat just until blended.

3 Pour the batter into the pan. Bake until a toothpick inserted into the center comes out clean, 20–25 minutes. Let cool completely in the pan on a rack. Run a thin knife around the edge of the cake to loosen it from the pan. Invert onto the rack; remove the wax paper.

4 With a serrated knife, cut the cake horizontally in half. Place 1 layer, cut side up, on a serving plate. With a narrow metal spatula, spread 2 cups of the ice cream over the cake in an even layer, spreading it all the way to the edges. (Make the layer as level as possible.) Freeze until firm, about 30 minutes. Spread the sorbet over the ice cream layer in an even layer; freeze until firm, about 30 minutes. Spread the remaining ice cream in an even layer on top of the sorbet; top with the remaining cake layer, cut side down. Wrap tightly in heavy-duty foil; freeze until completely frozen, at least 3 hours or up to 1 week.

5 Let the cake stand at room temperature 10 minutes. With a serrated knife, cut the cake in half, then cut each half crosswise into 6 slices. Place a slice on each of 12 chilled plates and serve at once.

PER SERVING (1/12 of cake): 217 Cal, 2 g Fat, 1 g Sat Fat, 0 g Trans Fat, 5 mg Chol, 175 mg Sod, 46 g Carb, 1 g Fib, 4 g Prot, 106 mg Calc. **POINTS** value: **4.**

Very Easy Baked Alaska

HANDS-ON PREP 30 MIN   COOK 5 MIN   SERVES 8

4   (¾-inch-thick) slices store-bought angel
    food cake
¼   cup orange or other fruit-flavored liqueur
    or orange juice
1   quart fat-free vanilla ice cream or flavor
    of choice
4   egg whites, at room temperature
Pinch salt
½   cup sugar
½   teaspoon vanilla extract

1 Using a 3-inch round cookie cutter, cut out 1 round from each slice of cake. Place the rounds on a plate and freeze until firm, about 1 hour. Place the cake rounds on a baking sheet about 3 inches apart and brush with the liqueur. Top each cake round with 1 large scoop (about 1 cup) of the ice cream. Cover tightly with plastic wrap and freeze until completely frozen, at least 30 minutes or up to overnight.

2 Position a rack in the middle of the oven and preheat the oven to 475°F.

3 With an electric mixer on medium-high speed, beat the egg whites and salt in a large bowl until soft peaks form. Add the sugar, about 1 tablespoon at a time, beating until stiff, glossy peaks form. Beat in the vanilla.

4 Quickly spread a generous cup of the meringue over each ice-cream cake. With a rubber spatula, create smooth domed tops, making sure the meringue completely covers the ice cream and cake. With the back of a small spoon, form swirls in the meringue starting at the tops of the domes. Immediately place in the oven and bake until the meringues are lightly browned, 4–5 minutes. Using a pancake spatula, transfer the desserts to a cutting board and cut in half. Transfer to each of 8 plates and serve at once.

PER SERVING (½ of one Baked Alaska): 186 Cal, 0 g Fat, 0 g Sat Fat, 0 g Trans Fat, 0 mg Chol, 169 mg Sod, 40 g Carb, 0 g Fib, 4 g Prot, 98 mg Calc. **POINTS** value: **4.**

Food Note   This impressive and surprisingly easy-to-prepare dessert has been enjoyed for over 200 years. Thomas Jefferson served it at the White House; his early version consisted of ice cream encased in a hot pastry crust. Baked Alaska really came into its own, however, when served at Delmonico's restaurant in New York City in 1876, to celebrate the purchase of the territory of Alaska.

Watermelon Bombe

HANDS-ON PREP 30 MIN   COOK 6 MIN   SERVES 12

1   cup water
⅓ cup sugar
1   (2-pound) piece watermelon, rind removed,
    seeded, and chopped
1   tablespoon fresh lime juice
1   quart reduced-fat pistachio ice cream, slightly
softened
1   pint fat-free vanilla ice cream, slightly softened
½ cup mini semisweet chocolate chips

1 To make the sugar syrup, combine the water and sugar in a small saucepan and set over high heat. Bring to a boil, stirring until the sugar is dissolved. Reduce the heat and simmer 5 minutes. Transfer the syrup to a small bowl; cover and refrigerate until thoroughly chilled, about 30 minutes.

2 Meanwhile, to make the watermelon sorbet, puree the watermelon, in batches, in a food processor, transferring each batch to a medium bowl. Pour the puree through a sieve set over a medium bowl, pressing hard on the solids to extract as much liquid as possible; discard the solids. Stir in the sugar syrup and lime juice. Transfer the watermelon mixture to an ice-cream maker and freeze according to the manufacturer's instructions. Transfer the sorbet to a bowl; cover and place in the freezer. Line a 3-quart bowl with 3 overlapping pieces of plastic wrap, keeping the wrap as wrinkle-free as possible and allowing the excess to extend over the rim by 4 inches. Freeze the bowl until very cold.

3 With a rubber spatula, spread the pistachio ice cream inside the bowl, making a ½-inch-thick wall. Freeze until completely frozen, about 30 minutes. Spread the vanilla ice cream in an even layer over the pistachio ice cream, making a layer about ¼ inch thick. Freeze until completely frozen, about 30 minutes.

4 Stir the chocolate chips into the watermelon sorbet and pack into the center of the mold. Cover tightly with the plastic wrap; wrap in heavy-duty foil. Freeze until completely frozen, at least 4 hours or up to 1 week.

5 Remove the foil. Fold back the plastic wrap and invert the bombe onto a serving plate. Lift off the bowl and remove the plastic wrap. With a serrated knife, cut the bombe into wedges and place on chilled plates. Serve at once. The bombe can also be unmolded and returned to the freezer until ready to serve or up to 4 hours.

PER SERVING (1/12 of bombe): 177 Cal, 6 g Fat, 3 g Sat Fat, 0 g Trans Fat, 16 mg Chol, 57 mg Sod, 30 g Carb, 1 g Fib, 3 g Prot, 101 mg Calc. **POINTS** value: *4.*

Hot Fudge Sundae Pie

HANDS-ON PREP 30 MIN   COOK 10 MIN   SERVES 16

CRUST

9 whole (2½ x 5-inch) chocolate graham crackers

2 tablespoons honey

1 tablespoon canola oil

1 tablespoon low-fat (1%) milk

FILLING

1 pint fat-free vanilla ice cream, slightly softened

1 pint fat-free coffee ice cream, slightly softened

1 pint fat-free chocolate ice cream, slightly softened

2 ounces bittersweet or semisweet chocolate, chopped

1 teaspoon canola oil

16 medium strawberries

World's Easiest Hot Fudge Sauce (page 197)

1 Preheat the oven to 375°F. Spray a 9-inch pie plate with nonstick spray.

2 To make the crust, put the graham crackers in a food processor and pulse until finely ground. Add the honey, oil, and milk; process until moist and crumbly. Press the crumb mixture evenly onto the bottom and up the side of the pie plate. Bake until firm, 8–10 minutes. Let cool completely, then freeze until firm, about 30 minutes.

3 To make the filling, with a narrow metal spatula, spread the vanilla ice cream in the crust to form an even layer. Place scoops of the coffee and chocolate ice creams on top of the vanilla ice cream. Loosely wrap the pie in wax paper and then in heavy-duty foil. Freeze until completely frozen, at least 4 hours or up to 1 week.

4 Fill a small saucepan with 1½ inches of water and set over medium-low heat; bring almost to a simmer. Combine the chocolate and oil in a small bowl and set over the saucepan; whisk until the chocolate is melted and the mixture is smooth. Remove the bowl from the saucepan. Line a baking sheet with wax paper. One at a time, dip the strawberries, two-thirds of the way into the chocolate; shake off any excess. Place on the wax paper. If the chocolate gets too cool, return the bowl briefly to the saucepan to heat it. Let the berries stand until the chocolate is set, about 30 minutes. Carefully lift the berries from the wax paper and place on a plate. Refrigerate up to 8 hours.

5 Let the pie soften slightly in the refrigerator about 15 minutes. Cut the pie into 16 wedges and place on chilled plates. Drizzle each serving with 3 tablespoons of the hot fudge sauce and garnish with a chocolate-dipped strawberry. Serve at once.

PER SERVING (¹⁄₁₆ of pie): 230 Cal, 10 g Fat, 6 g Sat Fat, 0 g Trans Fat, 1 mg Chol, 115 mg Sod, 36 g Carb, 2 g Fib, 4 g Prot, 101 mg Calc. **POINTS** value: **5.**

Layered Sorbet Terrine

HANDS-ON PREP 10 MIN   COOK NONE   SERVES 8

1   pint mango sorbet, slightly softened
1   pint lemon sorbet, slightly softened
1   pint raspberry sorbet, slightly softened
Fresh berries (optional)
Fresh mint sprigs (optional)

1 Line a 4½ x 8½-inch loaf pan with 2 sheets of plastic wrap, allowing the excess to extend over the rim by 2 inches.

2 With a rubber spatula, spread the mango sorbet evenly in the pan, packing it into the corners. Top with an even layer of the lemon sorbet, then the raspberry sorbet. Tightly wrap in plastic wrap and then in heavy-duty foil. Freeze until completely frozen, at least 5 hours or up to 1 week.

3 Remove the terrine from the freezer and let stand at room temperature about 5 minutes. Invert the terrine onto a cutting board. Lift off the pan and remove the foil and plastic wrap. With a thin, sharp knife, cut the terrine crosswise into 1-inch-thick slices and place on chilled plates. Garnish with berries and mint (if using) and serve at once.

PER SERVING (1 slice): 195 Cal, 0 g Fat, 0 g Sat Fat, 0 g Trans Fat, 0 mg Chol, 14 mg Sod, 52 g Carb, 1 g Fib, 0 g Prot, 6 mg Calc. *POINTS* value: *4.*

Good Idea   We love the flavor and color combination of the mango, lemon, and raspberry sorbets, but you can use any sorbets you like. Or use the same sorbet for the top and bottom layer and a different one for the middle.

10-Minute Sensations

Chapter 8

Strawberry-Blackberry Crush

HANDS-ON PREP 10 MIN   COOK NONE   SERVES 4

1   (6-ounce) container blackberries
1   tablespoon pure maple syrup
1   (16-ounce) package frozen whole
     strawberries, thawed slightly
1   cup coarsely crushed ice cubes
6   tablespoons sugar
¼   cup + 1 tablespoon sliced blanched almonds
1   teaspoon fresh lemon juice
1   teaspoon almond extract

1 Toss together the blackberries and maple syrup in a small bowl; set aside.

2 Put the strawberries, ice, sugar, ¼ cup of the almonds, the lemon juice, and almond extract in a food processor and puree. Immediately divide the mixture evenly among 4 wineglasses. Top evenly with the blackberry mixture and sprinkle with the remaining 1 tablespoon of almonds. Serve at once.

PER SERVING (generous ¾ cup crush, ¼ cup blackberries, and ¾ teaspoon almonds): 186 Cal, 4 g Fat, 0 g Sat Fat, 0 g Trans Fat, 0 mg Chol, 4 mg Sod, 38 g Carb, 5 g Fib, 3 g Prot, 51 mg Calc. **POINTS** value: *3.*

How We Did It   To crush ice, place the cubes in a zip-close plastic bag, seal, and coarsely crush with a rolling pin. To make the almonds even more tasty, toast them by putting them into a skillet and cooking until lightly golden, which will take about 5 minutes over medium heat.

STRAWBERRY-BLACKBERRY
CRUSH

Red and Blue Berries Jubilee

HANDS-ON PREP 5 MIN   COOK 2 MIN   SERVES 4

½ **cup blueberries**

½ **cup raspberries**

2 **tablespoons orange-flavored liqueur**

2 **tablespoons orange juice**

2 **tablespoons sugar**

1 **teaspoon cornstarch**

2 **cups vanilla fat-free frozen yogurt**

1 Toss together the blueberries, raspberries, and orange liqueur in a small bowl; set aside.

2 Combine the orange juice, sugar, and cornstarch in a small saucepan; add the blueberry mixture. Cook, stirring, until the mixture boils and thickens, about 1 minute. Remove the saucepan from the heat and let cool slightly.

3 Place a ½-cup scoop of the frozen yogurt into each of 4 goblets or dessert dishes. Spoon about ¼ cup of the berry mixture on top and serve at once.

PER SERVING (½ cup frozen yogurt and ¼ cup berry mixture): 176 Cal, 0 g Fat, 0 g Sat Fat, 0 g Trans Fat, 2 mg Chol, 68 mg Sod, 38 g Carb, 1 g Fib, 5 g Prot, 166 mg Calc. **POINTS** value: **3.**

Good Idea   Turn this dessert into a quick and satisfying breakfast or lunch. Spoon vanilla fat-free yogurt (not frozen) into a goblet, and alternately layer with the berry mixture and reduced-fat granola. Add fresh sliced peaches or nectarines, if you like. (¼ cup of berry mixture, ½ cup vanilla fat-free yogurt, and ¼ cup low-fat granola will give you a **POINTS** value of about **4).**

Strawberries and Cream Cupcakes

HANDS-ON PREP 10 MIN   COOK NONE   SERVES 4

¼ cup thawed frozen fat-free whipped topping
4   (2-ounce) plain sugar-free cupcakes
1½ cups strawberries, hulled
2   tablespoons granulated sugar
1   teaspoon fresh lemon juice
Confectioners' sugar

1 Fit a small pastry bag with a medium plain tip; fill with the whipped topping. Carefully insert the pastry tip into the top of a cupcake; pipe in about 1 tablespoon topping. Repeat with the remaining cupcakes and whipped topping. Place the cupcakes on a platter; set aside.

2 To make strawberry fans, put 4 strawberries, stem end down, on a cutting board. With a sharp knife, cut the strawberries into very thin slices, leaving the berries intact at the stem end. Fan the slices of each strawberry and place one on top of each cupcake. Place the cupcakes on plates. Slice the remaining strawberries; toss with the granulated sugar and lemon juice in a small bowl. Spoon the strawberry mixture around the cupcakes, dividing evenly. Dust the cupcakes with confectioners' sugar and serve at once.

PER SERVING (1 cupcake and ⅓ cup strawberries): 232 Cal, 9 g Fat, 5 g Sat Fat, 0 g Trans Fat, 55 mg Chol, 174 mg Sod, 40 g Carb, 1 g Fib, 4 g Prot, 82 mg Calc. *POINTS* value: **5.**

Good Idea   If you don't own a pastry bag, a zip-close plastic bag is the perfect substitute. Spoon the whipped topping into the bag and snip off one of the corners. Since the bag is disposable, cleanup will be a piece of cake!

Baby Pavlovas

1   (24-ounce) jar sliced mango
    in extra-light syrup
1   cup blueberries
1   (6-ounce) container blackberries
1   ripe medium banana, diced
1   kiwi fruit, peeled and diced
2   tablespoons pure maple syrup
1   tablespoon chopped fresh mint

6   3-inch store-bought or homemade
    meringue shells
6   tablespoons thawed frozen fat-free
    whipped topping
6   fresh mint sprigs

1 Drain the mango, reserving 2 tablespoons of the syrup. Dice enough of the mango to equal about 1/4 cup; set aside. Put the remaining mango and reserved syrup in a food processor and puree; set aside. Gently toss together the blueberries, blackberries, banana, kiwi, diced mango, maple syrup, and chopped mint in a medium bowl.

2 Drizzle about 3 tablespoons of the mango puree onto each of 6 plates; top with a meringue shell. Spoon about 1/2 cup of the fruit mixture into and around each shell and top with 1 tablespoon of the whipped topping. Garnish each with a mint sprig. Serve at once.

PER SERVING (1 dessert): 124 Cal, 1 g Fat, 0 g Sat Fat, 0 g Trans Fat, 0 mg Chol, 13 mg Sod, 31 g Carb, 3 g Fib, 1 g Prot, 27 mg Calc. **POINTS** value: **2.**

Try It   Individual meringue shells are sold in specialty food stores and in some bakeries.

Tropical Fool

HANDS-ON PREP 10 MIN   COOK NONE   SERVES 4

2 ripe medium bananas, cut into ½-inch
   chunks
2 cups (½-inch) diced ripe papaya
¼ cup orange juice
2 tablespoons confectioners' sugar
2 teaspoons fresh lime juice
1 cup thawed frozen fat-free whipped topping
2 tablespoons sweetened flaked coconut,
   toasted
2 tablespoons grated lime zest
   (about 2 large limes)

Put the bananas, papaya, orange juice, confectioners' sugar, and lime juice in a food processor and puree. Scrape into a medium bowl. With a rubber spatula, gently fold in the whipped topping until blended. Spoon into wineglasses or dessert dishes. Sprinkle with the toasted coconut and lime zest; serve at once.

PER SERVING (¾ cup): 140 Cal, 2 g Fat, 1 g Sat Fat, 0 g Trans Fat, 0 mg Chol, 15 mg Sod, 33 g Carb, 3 g Fib, 1 g Prot, 27 mg Calc. **POINTS** value: **2.**

Plan Ahead   If you prefer, puree the fruit mixture up to 2 hours ahead (the fruit juices will prevent the banana from browning).

Chilly Peach Melba Compote

HANDS-ON PREP 10 MIN   COOK NONE   SERVES 6

4   ripe medium peaches, cut into thin wedges
1   (6-ounce) container raspberries
3   tablespoons chilled rosé wine
1   tablespoon grated lime zest
1   tablespoon fresh lime juice
¼   cup ice-cold water
¼   cup superfine sugar
6   fresh mint sprigs

1 Combine the peaches, raspberries, wine, and lime zest and juice in a large bowl; set aside.

2 To make the sugar syrup, combine the ice-cold water and superfine sugar in a small bowl; stir until the sugar is dissolved. Add to the fruit mixture, gently tossing to combine. Spoon 1 cup of the compote into each of 6 chilled wineglasses or glass dessert dishes and garnish each with a mint sprig.

PER SERVING (1 cup): 75 Cal, 0 g Fat, 0 g Sat Fat, 0 g Trans Fat, 0 mg Chol, 1 mg Sod, 17 g Carb, 2 g Fib, 1 g Prot, 12 mg Calc. *POINTS* value: *1.*

Good Idea   Simple syrup is easy to make and good to have on hand. Use it to brush on cake layers for added moistness, toss it with fruit to balance out the fruit's acidity, or add it to chilled beverages, such as iced tea or coffee, for instant sweetening. No matter how much you make, the proportions are always the same: equal parts water and sugar. Refrigerated, sugar syrup will keep up to 2 weeks.

10-Minute Tiramisu

HANDS-ON PREP 10 MIN   COOK NONE   SERVES 6

¾ cup boiling water

2 teaspoons instant espresso powder

1 tablespoon dark rum or ½ teaspoon
rum extract

1 tablespoon sugar

1 (5-ounce) package sponge dessert shells

1½ (14-ounce) packages fat-free vanilla
pudding cups

¾ cup thawed frozen fat-free whipped topping

2 tablespoons grated semisweet chocolate
Unsweetened cocoa powder

1 Combine the boiling water, espresso powder, rum, and sugar in a small bowl; stir until the sugar and espresso powder are dissolved. Set aside to cool slightly.

2 Put a dessert shell on each of 6 dessert plates. Brush with the espresso mixture until saturated; set aside.

3 Put the pudding in a medium bowl. With a rubber spatula, gently fold in the whipped topping. Spread in each dessert shell, dividing evenly. Sprinkle with the grated chocolate and dust lightly with cocoa powder. Refrigerate until chilled, about 1 hour.

PER SERVING (1 tiramisu): 204 Cal, 2 g Fat, 1 g Sat Fat, 0 g Trans Fat, 39 mg Chol, 226 mg Sod, 43 g Carb, 0 g Fib, 4 g Prot, 68 mg Calc. *POINTS* value: *4.*

Good Idea   Make the tiramisu a day ahead to allow enough time for the sponge shells to absorb all of the delicious rum-espresso flavor. This is a great recipe when you need a fabulous dessert to serve a large number of people.

Cannoli Crisps

HANDS-ON PREP 10 MIN   COOK NONE   SERVES 4

½ **cup whole-milk ricotta cheese**
5 **tablespoons confectioners' sugar**
½ **teaspoon vanilla extract**
1 **teaspoon grated orange zest**
2 **tablespoons mini semisweet chocolate chips**
8 **pizzelle wafer cookies**
Confectioners' sugar

Stir together the ricotta, confectioners' sugar, vanilla, and orange zest in a small bowl. Stir in the chocolate chips. Spoon 2 tablespoons of the ricotta filling on each of 4 wafers. Top with the remaining 4 wafers to make sandwiches. Dust lightly with confectioners' sugar and serve at once.

PER SERVING (1 cannoli crisp): 167 Cal, 8 g Fat, 4 g Sat Fat, 0 g Trans Fat, 22 mg Chol, 54 mg Sod, 21 g Carb, 1 g Fib, 4 g Prot, 70 mg Calc. **POINTS** value: **4.**

Food Note   Pizzelle (peetz-ELL) are thin, crisp Italian wafer cookies that are cooked in a round cast-iron press similar to a waffle iron. Its intricately carved surfaces imprint a beautiful floral design onto both sides of the cookies. Pizzelle are often shaped into ice-cream cones while warm. Look for packaged pizzelle in the bakery department or ethnic food isle of larger supermarkets and in specialty food stores.

Easy Tartufo

HANDS-ON PREP 10 MIN   COOK NONE   SERVES 6

6 reduced-fat chocolate sandwich cookies,
    finely crushed
3 cups low-fat cherry vanilla ice cream
¾ cup light chocolate syrup

1 Line a small baking sheet with wax paper and scatter the crushed cookies on top; set aside.

2 Using a ½-cup ice-cream scoop, scoop the ice cream into 6 balls and place on a chilled baking sheet. Working quickly, roll the ice-cream balls, one at a time, in the crushed cookies until coated; return them to the chilled baking sheet. Freeze until firm, about 1 hour.

3 Put a sheet of wax paper under a rack. Remove the ice-cream balls from the freezer and transfer to the rack. Quickly spoon 2 tablespoons of the chocolate syrup over each ball, coating the top and sides. Place the rack with the ice-cream balls on a baking sheet and place in the freezer until firm, at least 1 hour or up to 4 hours. Let the tartufo stand at room temperature about 5 minutes before transferring to chilled plates for serving.

PER SERVING (1 tartufo): 212 Cal, 6 g Fat, 3 g Sat Fat, 0 g Trans Fat, 23 mg Chol, 144 mg Sod, 36 g Carb, 0 g Fib, 3 g Prot, 101 mg Calc. **POINTS** value: **5.**

How We Did It   To scoop ice cream quickly and easily, purchase it in a half-gallon rectangular carton. The length of the carton makes it easy to drag the scoop across the ice cream to form perfectly round balls.

Brownie Crunch Parfaits

HANDS-ON PREP 10 MIN   COOK NONE   SERVES 6

3   (3-ounce) fat-free brownies, cut into ½-inch
    cubes
½   cup fat-free raspberry fruit topping
¼   cup peanut brittle, coarsely chopped
½   cup thawed frozen fat-free whipped topping
6   (1-inch) pieces peanut brittle

Alternately layer one-sixth each of the brownie cubes, fruit topping, chopped peanut brittle, and whipped topping in each of 6 parfait glasses. Garnish each parfait with a piece of peanut brittle. Serve at once or cover and refrigerate up to 1 hour.

PER SERVING (1 parfait): 209 Cal, 3 g Fat, 1 g Sat Fat, 0 g Trans Fat, 0 mg Chol, 189 mg Sod, 45 g Carb, 2 g Fib, 3 g Prot, 27 mg Calc. *POINTS* value: *4.*

How We Did It   To easily cut the brownies into neat cubes, place them in the freezer for about 30 minutes, or until firm.

Chocolate–Marshmallow Fluff Squares

HANDS-ON PREP 10 MIN   **COOK** NONE   **SERVES** 8

- 8 **whole reduced-fat cinnamon graham crackers**
- 3 **tablespoons reduced-fat creamy peanut butter**
- 3 **tablespoons marshmallow crème**
- ¼ **cup semisweet chocolate chips, melted**
- 3 **tablespoons coarsely chopped peanuts**

1 Break each graham cracker in half to make 16 squares. Spread each of 8 squares with 1 rounded teaspoon peanut butter. Spread each of the remaining 8 squares with 1 rounded teaspoon marshmallow crème. Press the peanut butter and marshmallow squares together to form sandwiches; place on a wax paper–lined baking sheet.

2 Drizzle the melted chocolate over each sandwich in a zigzag pattern and sprinkle with the peanuts. Freeze until the chocolate is partially set, about 10 minutes.

PER SERVING (1 sandwich): 144 Cal, 6 g Fat, 2 g Sat Fat, 0 g Trans Fat, 0 mg Chol, 134 mg Sod, 20 g Carb, 2 g Fib, 4 g Prot, 23 mg Calc. *POINTS* value: *3.*

Good Idea   Milk chocolate or white chocolate chips can also be used for drizzling. Microwave them for a little less time, as they are more delicate than semisweet chocolate and melt more quickly.

Yogurt Cream with Dried Fruit and Nuts

HANDS-ON PREP 10 MIN   **COOK** NONE   **SERVES** 4

3   **cups plain reduced-fat Greek-style yogurt**

¼   **cup honey**

½   **cup dried tart cherries**

¼   **cup chopped pistachio nuts**

Divide the yogurt among 4 wineglasses or dessert dishes. Drizzle with the honey, then sprinkle with the cherries and pistachios. Serve at once.

Per serving (¾ cup yogurt, 1 tablespoon honey, 2 tablespoons dried cherries, and 1 tablespoon pistachios): 274 Cal, 6 g Fat, 2 g Sat Fat, 0 g Trans Fat, 11 mg Chol, 130 mg Sod, 46 g Carb, 3 g Fib, 12 g Prot, 356 mg Calc. **POINTS** value: **5.**

Good Idea   Make this dessert into breakfast by serving with reduced-fat toasted waffles or pancakes. (1 frozen reduced-fat waffle or pancake will increase the per-serving **POINTS** value by **1).**

Dessert Sauces

Chapter 9

Dark Chocolate Sauce

HANDS-ON PREP 8 MIN   COOK 6 MIN   SERVES 12   MAKES 2 CUPS

8   ounces bittersweet or semisweet chocolate,
    finely chopped
1   cup water
Pinch salt
¾   teaspoon vanilla extract

Fill a medium saucepan with 1½ inches of water and set over medium-low heat; bring to a slow simmer. Combine the chocolate, water, and salt in a medium bowl and set over the saucepan; whisk until the chocolate is melted and the mixture is smooth. Remove the bowl from the saucepan; whisk in the vanilla. Use immediately, or cool to room temperature. Transfer the sauce to a covered container; refrigerate up to 1 month. Stir well to serve chilled or gently reheat.

PER SERVING (about 2½ tablespoons): 88 Cal, 6 g Fat, 4 g Sat Fat, 0 g Trans Fat, 0 mg Chol, 25 mg Sod, 10 g Carb, 1 g Fib, 1 g Prot, 10 mg Calc. **POINTS** value: **2.**

Good Idea   For a deep dark mocha-flavored sauce, substitute 1 cup of strong brewed coffee for the water.

World's Easiest Hot Fudge Sauce

HANDS-ON PREP 10 MIN   COOK 6 MIN   SERVES 12   MAKES 1½ CUPS

1   cup fat-free half-and-half
2   tablespoons light corn syrup
Pinch salt
8   ounces bittersweet or semisweet chocolate,
    finely chopped
½   teaspoon vanilla extract

1 Combine the half-and-half, corn syrup, and salt in a heavy medium saucepan and set over medium-high heat. Bring just to a boil, whisking until smooth. Remove the saucepan from the heat. Whisk in the chocolate until melted and smooth.

2 Return the mixture to a boil, whisking constantly; boil about 1 minute. Remove the saucepan from the heat and whisk in the vanilla. Use immediately, or cool to room temperature. Transfer to a covered container; refrigerate up to 1 month. Gently reheat before serving.

PER SERVING (2 tablespoons): 114 Cal, 7 g Fat, 4 g Sat Fat, 0 g Trans Fat, 1 mg Chol, 58 mg Sod, 15 g Carb, 2 g Fib, 2 g Prot, 29 mg Calc. *POINTS* value: **2.**

Good Idea   This fabulous sauce tastes delicious over almost any ice cream or frozen yogurt. Of course it is delicious when spooned over Fresh Mint–Chocolate-Chip Ice Cream (page 168) or Frozen Vanilla-Bean Yogurt (page 163), but why not try it over something a little unexpected, such as the Roasted Banana and Pecan Ice Cream (page 167) for a truly luscious experience.

APPLE-CIDER BAKED APPLES,
PAGE 112, WITH
RICH AND CREAMY
BUTTERSCOTCH SAUCE

Rich and Creamy Butterscotch Sauce

HANDS-ON PREP 10 MIN   COOK 8 MIN   SERVES 12   MAKES 1½ CUPS

1   cup packed dark brown sugar
½   cup fat-free half-and-half
⅓   cup light corn syrup
1   tablespoon unsalted butter
1   teaspoon apple-cider vinegar
Pinch salt
½   teaspoon vanilla extract

Combine the brown sugar, half-and-half, corn syrup, butter, vinegar, and salt in a medium saucepan and set over medium heat. Bring to a boil, whisking, until the sugar is dissolved. Reduce the heat and simmer 2 minutes. Remove the saucepan from the heat and stir in the vanilla. Cool slightly to serve warm, or transfer to a covered container; refrigerate up to 1 week. Gently reheat before serving.

PER SERVING (2 tablespoons): 111 Cal, 1 g Fat, 1 g Sat Fat, 0 g Trans Fat, 3 mg Chol, 51 mg Sod, 26 g Carb, 0 g Fib, 0 g Prot, 27 mg Calc. **POINTS** value: **2.**

Good Idea   This sauce is delicious over baked apples, but it also makes a fabulous butterscotch sundae. Here's how: place a couple of scoops of Frozen Vanilla-Bean Yogurt (page 163) in a dish, top with a dollop of fat-free whipped topping, drizzle with 2 tablespoons butterscotch sauce, and garnish with a sprinkling of chopped toasted hazelnuts.

Chocolate Caramel Sauce

HANDS-ON PREP 6 MIN   COOK 20 MIN   SERVES 16   MAKES 2 CUPS

4   ounces bittersweet or semisweet chocolate,
    finely chopped
1   cup warm water
Pinch salt
1   cup fat-free half-and-half
2   cups sugar
2   tablespoons light corn syrup

1 Fill a medium saucepan with 1½ inches of water and set over medium-low heat; bring to a slow simmer. Combine the chocolate, ¼ cup of the warm water, and the salt in a medium bowl; set over the saucepan. Whisk until the chocolate is melted and the mixture is smooth. Remove the bowl from the saucepan; set aside. Pour out the water in the saucepan.

2 Pour the half-and-half into the same saucepan and set over medium heat; heat just until hot, about 3 minutes. Remove the saucepan from the heat; set aside.

3 Combine the sugar, the remaining ¾ cup of warm water, and the corn syrup in a large heavy saucepan. Cook over medium heat, stirring, until the sugar is dissolved. Increase the heat to high. Bring to a boil, washing down the side of the pan with a pastry brush dipped into cool water to dissolve any sugar crystals. Boil, without stirring, until the caramel turns a rich golden brown.

4 Immediately remove the saucepan from the heat. Wearing long oven mitts to protect your arms and being careful to avoid any spatters, whisk in the half-and-half, about 2 tablespoons at a time. Set the saucepan over low heat and cook, whisking constantly, until the sauce is smooth. Remove the saucepan from the heat; pour in the chocolate mixture and whisk until smooth. Use immediately, or cool to room temperature. Transfer to a covered container; refrigerate up to 1 month. Gently reheat the sauce before serving, adding a little water to thin the sauce slightly, if necessary.

PER SERVING (2 tablespoons): 148 Cal, 3 g Fat, 2 g Sat Fat, 0 g Trans Fat, 1 mg Chol, 43 mg Sod, 32 g Carb, 1 g Fib, 1 g Prot, 19 mg Calc. *POINTS* value: *3.*

Custard Sauce

HANDS-ON PREP 5 MIN   COOK 15 MIN   SERVES 14   MAKES 3½ CUPS

2   **cups fat-free half-and-half**
1   **cup fat-free egg substitute**
½   **cup sugar**
Pinch salt
¾   **teaspoon vanilla extract**

1 Bring the half-and-half just to a boil in a medium saucepan set over medium heat.

2 Meanwhile, whisk together the egg substitute, sugar, and salt in a medium bowl. Slowly add ½ cup of the hot half-and-half mixture, whisking constantly. Return the mixture to the saucepan and set over medium-low heat. Cook, whisking constantly, until the custard thickens and coats the back of a spoon, about 5 minutes. (Do not let boil.)

3 Immediately pour the custard through a fine-mesh sieve set over a medium bowl. Let cool to room temperature, whisking occasionally. Whisk in the vanilla. Serve warm, or transfer to a covered container and refrigerate up to 4 days. Serve chilled, or gently reheat to serve warm.

PER SERVING (¼ cup): 50 Cal, 0 g Fat, 0 g Sat Fat, 0 g Trans Fat, 2 mg Chol, 90 mg Sod, 9 g Carb, 0 g Fib, 2 g Prot, 34 mg Calc. **POINTS** value: **1.**

Food Note   If you like your custard sauce to contain the aromatic and flavorful black seeds of a vanilla bean, you have two options: Cut the vanilla bean in half lenghtwise and scrape out enough seeds to equal ¾ teaspoon. Or use vanilla bean paste, available in 4-ounce jars in specialty food stores.

Silky Strawberry Sauce

HANDS-ON PREP 8 MIN   COOK 10 MIN   SERVES 8   MAKES 2 CUPS

1   (1-pound) container strawberries,
     hulled and sliced
¼   cup light corn syrup
¼   cup water
Pinch salt
2   teaspoons fresh lemon juice

1 Combine the strawberries, corn syrup, water, and salt in a large saucepan and set over medium heat. Cook, stirring occasionally, until the berries soften and the mixture forms a sauce, about 10 minutes. Stir in the lemon juice.

2 Pour the berry mixture through a fine-mesh sieve set over a medium bowl, pressing hard on the solids to extract as much liquid as possible; discard the solids. Cool the sauce to serve at room temperature, or transfer to a covered container; refrigerate up to 1 week.

PER SERVING (¼ cup): 47 Cal, 0 g Fat, 0 g Sat Fat, 0 g Trans Fat, 0 mg Chol, 43 mg Sod, 12 g Carb, 1 g Fib, 0 g Prot, 10 mg Calc. *POINTS* value: *1.*

How We Did It   Strawberry seeds are really tiny, and it takes a very fine sieve to separate out the seeds to get a silky smooth sauce. Raspberries and blackberries which have much larger seeds, can be strained through a coarse sieve.

Blueberry Sauce

HANDS-ON PREP 6 MIN   COOK 5 MIN   SERVES 6   MAKES 1½ CUPS

2   cups fresh or frozen blueberries
½   cup confectioners' sugar
2   tablespoons water
Pinch salt
Pinch cinnamon (optional)
2   teaspoons fresh lemon juice

Combine the blueberries, confectioners' sugar, water, salt, and cinnamon (if using) in a large saucepan and set over medium heat. Cook, stirring occasionally, until the berries soften and the mixture forms a sauce, 5–7 minutes. Stir in the lemon juice. Serve at once, or let cool to room temperature. Refrigerate in a covered container up to 1 week. Just before using, shake the sauce well and serve chilled or gently reheat.

PER SERVING (¼ cup): 67 Cal, 0 g Fat, 0 g Sat Fat, 0 g Trans Fat, 0 mg Chol, 48 mg Sod, 17 g Carb, 1 g Fib, 0 g Prot, 3 mg Calc. **POINTS** value: **1.**

Good Idea   Double your blueberry pleasure by serving this sauce with the Lemon-Blueberry Pound Cake (page 18), or spoon around Buttermilk Panna Cotta, (page 137).

Fresh Raspberry-Orange Sauce

HANDS-ON PREP 12 MIN   COOK NONE   SERVES 8   MAKES SCANT 2 CUPS

3   (6-ounce) containers raspberries
⅛   teaspoon grated orange zest
⅓   cup confectioners' sugar
2   tablespoons fresh orange juice
1   teaspoon fresh lemon juice

1 Combine the raspberries and orange zest in a food processor; pulse just until the berries are broken up. Sift the confectioners' sugar over the berries and add the orange juice; pulse just until smooth.

2 Pour the berry mixture through a sieve set over a medium bowl, pressing hard on the solids to extract as much liquid as possible; discard the solids. Stir in the lemon juice. Transfer the sauce to a glass jar; refrigerate up to 1 week. Just before serving, shake well. The sauce may thicken a bit on standing; add a little orange juice or water to thin to the desired consistency.

PER SERVING (scant ¼ cup): 45 Cal, 0 g Fat, 0 g Sat Fat, 0 g Trans Fat, 0 mg Chol, 1 mg Sod, 11 g Carb, 1 g Fib, 1 g Prot, 12 mg Calc. **POINTS** value: **1.**

Food Note   It is important not to overprocess the raspberries, as the longer they are processed the greater the chance that the seeds will break open and release their slightly bitter flavor. Serve with Chocolate-Raspberry Soufflé Cakes.

CHOCOLATE-RASPBERRY
SOUFFLÉ CAKES, PAGE 28, WITH
FRESH RASPBERRY-ORANGE SAUCE

Bing Cherry–Brown Sugar Sauce

HANDS-ON PREP 8 MIN   COOK 10 MIN   SERVES 6   MAKES 1½ CUPS

1   tablespoon unsalted butter
2   cups Bing or other sweet cherries (about
     12 ounces), pitted
2   tablespoons packed light brown sugar
2   teaspoons fresh lemon juice
Pinch salt

Melt the butter in a medium nonstick skillet set over medium heat. Add the cherries and cook, stirring frequently, until they begin to release their juice, 3–5 minutes. Stir in the brown sugar, lemon juice, and salt. Bring to a boil over high heat. Reduce the heat and simmer, stirring occasionally, until the sugar dissolves and the juices thicken slightly, about 4 minutes. Remove the skillet from the heat; cool slightly to serve warm, or transfer to a covered container; refrigerate up to 2 days. Gently reheat to serve.

PER SERVING (¼ cup): 67 Cal, 2 g Fat, 1 g Sat Fat, 0 g Trans Fat, 5 mg Chol, 50 mg Sod, 13 g Carb, 1 g Fib, 1 g Prot, 11 mg Calc. **POINTS** value: **1.**

Express Lane   If you'd like to serve the sauce cold or at room temperature, replace the butter with an equal amount of flavorless canola oil, which enables the sauce to retain its silky texture. It is delicious spooned over thick slices of angel food cake.

Kumquat Sauce with Star Anise

HANDS-ON PREP 15 MIN   COOK 12 MIN   SERVES 6   MAKES 1½ CUPS

1   cup water
½   cup sugar
4   whole star anise
1   pound kumquats (about 40), thinly sliced,
    seeds discarded
Pinch salt

Combine the water and sugar in a medium saucepan and set over medium heat. Bring to a boil, stirring, until the sugar is dissolved. Add the star anise and return the mixture to a boil; boil 5 minutes. Stir in the kumquats and salt; simmer until slightly thickened, about 5 minutes. Remove the star anise and reserve for garnish, if desired. Use immediately, or cool to room temperature. Transfer to a covered container; refrigerate up to 1 week. Serve chilled or gently reheat.

PER SERVING (¼ cup): 119 Cal, 1 g Fat, 0 g Sat Fat, 0 g Trans Fat, 0 mg Chol, 56 mg Sod, 29 g Carb, 5 g Fib, 1 g Prot, 50 mg Calc. *POINTS* value: *2.*

How We Did It   We find that the easiest way to seed kumquats is to use a small pointed paring knife to pick out the seeds from the kumquat slices. Spoon over Frozen Vanilla-Bean Yogurt (page 163) or Classic New York–Style Cheesecake (page 29).

Desserts that Cut the Sugar

Chapter 10

Fresh Carrot–Ginger Cake

HANDS-ON PREP 25 MIN   COOK 35 MIN   SERVES 12

¾ cup whole-wheat flour

½ cup cake flour

¾ teaspoon cinnamon

¾ teaspoon baking powder

½ teaspoon baking soda

¼ teaspoon nutmeg

⅛ teaspoon ground allspice

¼ teaspoon salt

¼ cup + 2 tablespoons fat-free egg substitute

2 tablespoons packed sucralose–brown sugar blend

½ teaspoon vanilla extract

¼ cup unsweetened applesauce

¼ cup canola oil

2 tablespoons finely chopped crystallized ginger

½ pound carrots, coarsely shredded

¾ cup light cream cheese (Neufchâtel), softened

4½ teaspoons sucralose

1 Preheat the oven to 350°F. Lightly spray an 8-inch square baking pan with nonstick spray.

2 Whisk together the whole-wheat flour, cake flour, cinnamon, baking powder, baking soda, nutmeg, allspice, and salt in a medium bowl; set aside. With an electric mixer on medium-high speed, beat the egg substitute, sucralose–brown sugar blend, and vanilla until well blended, about 3 minutes. Add the applesauce and beat until combined. Gradually add the oil, beating until the mixture is frothy, about 3 minutes. Beat in the ginger. With a rubber spatula, stir in the flour mixture until just a little of the flour is still visible. Gently stir in the carrots just until combined.

3 Pour the batter into the pan. Bake until a toothpick inserted into the center comes out clean, about 35 minutes. Let cool completely in the pan on a rack.

4 Meanwhile, to make the frosting, with an electric mixer on medium-high speed, beat the cream cheese and sucralose in a small bowl until smooth and creamy, 2–3 minutes. With a narrow metal spatula, spread the frosting over the top of the cake. Serve at room temperature or refrigerate, covered, up to 2 days. Let stand at room temperature about 30 minutes before serving.

PER SERVING (¹⁄₁₂ of cake): 114 Cal, 4 g Fat, 2 g Sat Fat, 0 g Trans Fat, 11 mg Chol, 221 mg Sod, 16 g Carb, 2 g Fib, 4 g Prot, 44 mg Calc. **POINTS** value: **2.**

Express Lane   To save time, use peeled baby-cut carrots and shred them in a food processor using the coarse shredding disk. The carrots can be peeled and shredded a day ahead and stored in a zip-close plastic bag in the refrigerator. The flour mixture can be whisked together and stored in a plastic bag up to 2 days ahead.

Chocolate Cake with Banana Cream

HANDS-ON PREP 25 MIN   COOK 15 MIN   SERVES 12

- ⅔ cup whole-wheat pastry flour
- ½ cup sucralose
- ⅓ cup + 1 teaspoon unsweetened cocoa powder
- 1 tablespoon packed light brown sugar
- 1 teaspoon baking powder
- ¼ teaspoon salt
- 1 large egg
- ⅓ cup canola oil
- ¼ cup water

- 2 teaspoons vanilla extract
- ⅓ cup unsweetened applesauce
- 1 cup thawed frozen fat-free whipped topping
- 1 medium banana, sliced

1 Preheat the oven to 350°F. Lightly spray an 8-inch round cake pan with nonstick spray.

2 Whisk together the pastry flour, sucralose, ⅓ cup of the cocoa, the brown sugar, baking powder, and salt in a medium bowl; set aside. Whisk together the egg, oil, water, and vanilla in a separate medium bowl. Whisk in the applesauce until slightly frothy. With a rubber spatula, fold the flour mixture into the applesauce mixture just until blended.

3 Pour the batter into the pan. Bake until a toothpick inserted into the center comes out clean, about 15 minutes. Let cool completely in the pan on a rack.

4 Meanwhile, stir together the whipped topping and the remaining 1 teaspoon of cocoa in a small bowl until blended; fold in the banana. Cut the cake into 12 wedges; place a wedge on each of 12 plates. Top each wedge with 1 tablespoon of the banana cream.

PER SERVING (¹⁄₁₂ of cake): 115 Cal, 7 g Fat, 1 g Sat Fat, 0 g Trans Fat, 18 mg Chol, 98 mg Sod, 13 g Carb, 2 g Fib, 2 g Prot, 33 mg Calc. **POINTS** value: **2.**

How We Did It   Make sure you don't overmix the batter when the dry ingredients are added or the cake will develop a heavy texture. This cake is also delicious served warm with the banana cream on the side.

Orange Chiffon Cake with Bittersweet Chocolate Glaze

HANDS-ON PREP 25 MIN   COOK 50 MIN   SERVES 12

1   cup cake flour
8   tablespoons sucralose-sugar blend
2   teaspoons baking powder
½   teaspoon salt
2   large eggs
2   tablespoons grated orange zest
    (about 2 oranges)
¾   cup fresh orange juice
¼   cup canola oil

1   teaspoon brandy or orange-flavored liqueur
    (optional)
6   egg whites, at room temperature
½   teaspoon cream of tartar
2   ounces bittersweet chocolate

1 Place an oven rack in the lower third of the oven and preheat the oven to 325°F.

2 Whisk together the cake flour, 6 tablespoons of the sucralose-sugar blend, the baking powder, and salt in a large bowl. With an electric mixer on medium speed, add the eggs, orange zest and juice, oil, and brandy (if using) to the flour mixture and beat until well blended; set aside.

3 With clean beaters and with the mixer on medium speed, beat the egg whites and cream of tartar in a large bowl until soft peaks form. Increase the speed to high. Add the remaining 2 tablespoons of sucralose-sugar blend and beat until stiff peaks form. With a rubber spatula, fold one-fourth of the beaten whites into batter. Gently fold in the remaining whites just until no streaks of white remain.

4 Pour the batter into an ungreased nonstick 10-inch tube pan; spread evenly. Bake until a toothpick inserted into the center comes out clean, 50–55 minutes. (Do not open the oven door during the first 45 minutes of baking.) Invert the pan onto its legs or onto the neck of a bottle; let cool completely. Run a thin knife around the cake to loosen it from the side and center tube of the pan. Remove the cake from the pan and place, right side up, on a serving plate.

5 To make the chocolate glaze, place the chocolate in small microwavable bowl. Microwave on High 30 seconds; stir. Microwave until the chocolate is melted, 10–15 seconds longer. Cut the cake into 12 slices and place on plates. Drizzle each slice with some of the melted chocolate and serve at once. The cake can be wrapped in plastic wrap and stored at room temperature up 2 days or refrigerated up to 5 days.

PER SERVING (1/12 of cake and 1 teaspoon chocolate glaze): 165 Cal, 7 g Fat, 2 g Sat Fat, 0 g Trans Fat, 35 mg Chol, 219 mg Sod, 22 g Carb, 1 g Fib, 4 g Prot, 57 mg Calc. **POINTS** value: **4.**

ORANGE CHIFFON CAKE WITH
BITTERSWEET CHOCOLATE GLAZE

Cranberry-Walnut Loaf

HANDS-ON PREP 15 MIN   COOK 45 MIN   SERVES 12

1⅓ cups all-purpose flour

¾ cup whole-wheat flour

¼ cup sucralose

1 teaspoon baking powder

½ teaspoon baking soda

1¾ cups unsweetened apple juice

¼ cup fat-free egg substitute

3 tablespoons canola oil

2 teaspoons grated lemon zest

1½ teaspoons vanilla extract

¼ cup dried cranberries, chopped

¼ cup walnuts, chopped

1 tablespoon sesame seeds

1 Preheat the oven to 350°F. Lightly spray a 5 x 9-inch loaf pan with nonstick spray.

2 Whisk together the all-purpose flour, whole-wheat flour, sucralose, baking powder, and baking soda in a large bowl. Make a well in the center of the mixture.

3 Whisk together the apple juice, egg substitute, oil, lemon zest, and vanilla in a large measuring cup. Pour into the well in the flour mixture. With a wooden spoon, stir just until the flour mixture is moistened. Stir in the cranberries and walnuts.

4 Scrape the batter into the pan and spread evenly; sprinkle with the sesame seeds. Bake until a toothpick inserted into the center comes out clean, 45–50 minutes. Let cool in the pan on a rack 10 minutes. Remove the loaf from the pan and let cool completely on the rack.

PER SERVING (¹⁄₁₂ of cake): 154 Cal, 5 g Fat, 0 g Sat Fat, 0 g Trans Fat, 0 mg Chol, 105 mg Sod, 23 g Carb, 2 g Fib, 4 g Prot, 36 mg Calc. **POINTS** value: **3.**

Good Idea   For a variation, you can substitute grated orange zest for the lemon zest.

Apple-Walnut Crisp with Ginger Cream

HANDS-ON PREP 20 MIN   COOK 45 MIN   SERVES 8

5   cups (½-inch) diced peeled apples, such
    as McIntosh (about 3 large)
1   tablespoon pure maple syrup
2   teaspoons vanilla extract
½   teaspoon + pinch cinnamon
⅓   cup rolled (old-fashioned) oats
⅓   cup vanilla or plain puffed wheat cereal
¼   cup walnuts, chopped
2   tablespoons whole-wheat flour
1   tablespoon packed sucralose–brown sugar
    blend

1   tablespoon unsalted butter, softened
¼   cup water
½   cup thawed frozen fat-free whipped topping
¼   teaspoon ground ginger

1 Preheat the oven to 375°F.

2 Stir together the apples, maple syrup, vanilla, and ½ teaspoon of the cinnamon in a large bowl. Spread in an ungreased 8-inch square baking pan or 8-cup baking dish.

3 Stir together the oats, cereal, walnuts, whole-wheat flour, and sucralose–brown sugar blend in a medium bowl. With your fingers, blend in the butter until crumbly. Scatter over the fruit and sprinkle with the remaining pinch of cinnamon. Pour the water evenly over the oat mixture. Bake until the fruit filling is bubbly and the topping is a light golden brown, 45–50 minutes. Let cool in the pan on a rack.

4 Meanwhile, to make the ginger cream, stir together the whipped topping and ginger in a small bowl. Spoon the crisp evenly into 8 dessert dishes and spoon the ginger cream on top. Serve warm.

PER SERVING (⅛ of crisp and 1 tablespoon ginger cream): 118 Cal, 4 g Fat, 1 g Sat Fat, 0 g Trans Fat, 4 mg Chol, 4 mg Sod, 20 g Carb, 3 g Fib, 2 g Prot, 17 mg Calc. **POINTS** value: **2.**

Good Idea   To add a bit of complexity of flavor to this classic dessert, substitute a tart Granny Smith apple for one of the McIntosh apples.

MIXED BERRY
STRUDEL
WITH YOGURT
TOPPING

Mixed Berry Strudel with Yogurt Topping

HANDS-ON PREP 20 MIN   COOK 18 MIN   SERVES 8

3   cups mixed berries, such as blueberries,
    raspberries, blackberries, or diced strawberries
2   tablespoons instant tapioca
1   teaspoon grated lemon zest
5   (12 x 17-inch) sheets frozen phyllo dough,
    thawed
1½ tablespoons unsalted butter, melted
4   teaspoons ground walnuts or plain dried
    bread crumbs

½   cup plain fat-free Greek-style yogurt
½   teaspoon packed sucralose–brown sugar
    blend or 1 teaspoon packed brown sugar

1 Place an oven rack in the lower third of the oven and preheat the oven to 450°F. Lightly spray a baking sheet with nonstick spray.

2 Gently toss together the berries, tapioca, and lemon zest in a medium bowl; let stand 10 minutes.

3 Meanwhile, place a large sheet of parchment or wax paper on a work surface. Place a phyllo sheet on top, with a long side facing you. Keep the remaining phyllo covered with a damp towel and plastic wrap to prevent it from drying out. Lightly brush the phyllo sheets with the melted butter and sprinkle with about 1 teaspoon walnuts. Repeat with the remaining phyllo, butter, and walnuts to make 4 more layers.

4 Spoon the berry mixture over the phyllo in a lengthwise 3-inch-wide strip, leaving a 2½-inch border on the short sides and the long side nearest you. Fold the short sides of the phyllo over the filling, then roll up jelly-roll style. Place, seam side down, on the baking sheet and brush with the remaining butter. Bake until deep golden brown, 18–20 minutes. Let cool on the baking sheet on a rack until warm, about 20 minutes.

5 Meanwhile, to make the topping, combine the yogurt and sucralose–brown sugar blend. With a serrated knife, cut the strudel into 8 slices. Place the slices on a platter and serve the yogurt topping alongside.

PER SERVING (⅛ of strudel and 1 tablespoon yogurt): 108 Cal, 3 g Fat, 1 g Sat Fat, 0 g Trans Fat, 6 mg Chol, 58 mg Sod, 18 g Carb, 3 g Fib, 3 g Prot, 45 mg Calc. *POINTS* value: *2.*

Food Note Greek-style yogurt contains much less whey (the watery liquid that separates away) than American-style yogurts, resulting in yogurt with the rich consistency of sour cream. To turn regular yogurt into Greek-style yogurt, put plain fat-free yogurt in a fine-mesh sieve lined with 3 or 4 layers of cheesecloth or coffee filters and set over a bowl. Cover and refrigerate for 24 hours.

Strawberry Shortcakes

HANDS-ON PREP 20 MIN   COOK 14 MIN   SERVES 6

½ cup + 2 tablespoons whole-wheat flour

½ cup all-purpose flour

2 tablespoons + ¼ teaspoon sucralose

1 teaspoon baking powder

¼ teaspoon baking soda

1 tablespoon grated orange zest (about 1 orange)

1½ tablespoons unsalted butter, melted

1 cup + 6 tablespoons plain fat-free Greek-style yogurt, at room temperature

½ teaspoon vanilla extract

6 strawberries, hulled and sliced

1 Preheat the oven to 425°F. Lightly spray a baking sheet with nonstick spray.

2 Whisk together ½ cup of the whole-wheat flour, the all-purpose flour, 2 tablespoons of the sucralose, the baking powder, and baking soda in a large bowl. With a wooden spoon, stir in the orange zest, then the melted butter until the mixture is crumbly. Slowly stir 1 cup of the yogurt into the flour mixture until a dough forms.

3 Sprinkle the remaining 2 tablespoons of whole-wheat flour on a work surface. Shape the dough into a ball and lightly knead 6 times, incorporating as much of the flour as needed to keep the dough from sticking. Pat the dough to a ½-inch thickness. With a 3-inch round cookie cutter, cut out 4 biscuits, cutting straight down. Gather the dough scraps; reroll and cut out 2 more biscuits.

4 Place the biscuits on the baking sheet about 2 inches apart. Bake until golden, 14–16 minutes. Let cool on the baking sheet on a rack 5 minutes.

5 Meanwhile, to make the topping, combine the remaining 6 tablespoons of yogurt, the remaining ¼ teaspoon of sucralose, and the vanilla in a small bowl. Split the shortcakes; place the bottom halves on plates. Top each with one-sixth of the strawberries and 1 tablespoon of the yogurt mixture. Cover with the tops of the shortcakes and serve at once.

PER SERVING (1 filled shortcake): 144 Cal, 3 g Fat, 2 g Sat Fat, 0 g Trans Fat, 9 mg Chol, 178 mg Sod, 23 g Carb, 2 g Fib, 6 g Prot, 167 mg Calc. *POINTS* value: *3.*

Dried Cherry–Oatmeal Cookies

HANDS-ON PREP 15 MIN   COOK 12 MIN   MAKES 12

¾ cup rolled (old-fashioned) oats

¼ cup whole-wheat pastry flour

¼ teaspoon cinnamon

⅛ teaspoon baking soda

⅛ teaspoon salt

2 tablespoons unsalted butter, softened

2 tablespoons packed sucralose–brown sugar blend

1 tablespoon dark molasses

1 large egg

1 tablespoon water

¼ cup dried tart cherries

1 Preheat the oven to 350°F. Line a baking sheet with parchment paper.

2 Stir together the oats, pastry flour, cinnamon, baking soda, and salt in a medium bowl; set aside. With an electric mixer on medium speed, beat the butter and sucralose–brown sugar blend in a large bowl until light and fluffy, about 2 minutes. Add the molasses, egg, and water; beat until smooth, about 4 minutes. With a wooden spoon, stir in the oat mixture and dried cherries.

3 Drop the dough by generous tablespoonfuls on the baking sheet about 2½ inches apart, making a total of 12 cookies. Bake until the edges are golden and the centers are just set, about 12 minutes. Let cool completely on the baking sheet on a rack. Store in an airtight container in the refrigerator up to 4 days.

PER SERVING (1 cookie): 73 Cal, 3 g Fat, 1 g Sat Fat, 0 g Trans Fat, 23 mg Chol, 43 mg Sod, 11 g Carb, 1 g Fib, 2 g Prot, 14 mg Calc. **POINTS** value: **2.**

Good Idea   Just about any small or cut-up dried fruit would be delicious in these cookies. Try raisins, dried blueberries, or diced dried strawberries. If you are in the mood for a simpler—but equally delicious—oat cookie, omit the dried fruit.

Chocolate Crinkle Cookies

HANDS-ON PREP 10 MIN   COOK 10 MIN   MAKES 12

½ cup all-purpose flour
2 tablespoons whole-wheat pastry flour
⅓ cup packed sucralose–brown sugar blend
¼ cup unsweetened cocoa powder
½ teaspoon baking powder
⅛ teaspoon salt
2 tablespoons unsalted butter, softened
2 egg whites, lightly beaten
½ teaspoon vanilla extract
2½ teaspoons confectioners' sugar

1 Preheat the oven to 350°F. Spray a baking sheet with nonstick spray.

2 Whisk together the all-purpose flour, pastry flour, sucralose–brown sugar blend, cocoa, baking powder, and salt in a medium bowl. With a wooden spoon, stir in the butter until the mixture is well combined and crumbly. Add the egg whites and vanilla; stir until a smooth dough forms (you may need to use your hands).

3 Put the confectioners' sugar in a small bowl. Divide the dough into 12 equal pieces and roll each into a ball. Lightly roll each ball in the confectioners' sugar to coat. Place on the baking sheet about 2 inches apart. Bake until set but still soft in the middle, 10–12 minutes. Transfer the cookies to a rack and let cool completely. Store in an airtight container in the refrigerator up to 4 days.

PER SERVING (1 cookie): 70 Cal, 2 g Fat, 1 g Sat Fat, 0 g Trans Fat, 5 mg Chol, 56 mg Sod, 12 g Carb, 1 g Fib, 2 g Prot, 20 mg Calc. *POINTS* value: *1.*

Try It   This versatile cookie can be turned into a tasty, crunchy low-fat dessert topping: coarsely crush a cookie and sprinkle it over fat-free frozen yogurt.

CHOCOLATE CRINKLE
COOKIES

Espresso-Glazed Chocolate Brownies

HANDS-ON PREP 20 MIN   COOK 9 MIN   MAKES 12

¼ cup whole-wheat pastry flour

¼ cup all-purpose flour

½ teaspoon baking powder

⅛ teaspoon salt

3 tablespoons boiling water

¾ teaspoon instant espresso powder

3 tablespoons Dutch-process cocoa powder

1 tablespoon vanilla extract

1 ounce semisweet or bittersweet chocolate

2 tablespoons canola oil

3 tablespoons packed sucralose–brown sugar blend

1 large egg, beaten

¼ cup chopped walnuts (optional)

¾ teaspoon fat-free milk, heated

2 tablespoons confectioners' sugar

1 Preheat the oven to 350°F. Lightly spray an 8-inch square baking pan with nonstick spray.

2 Whisk together the pastry flour, all-purpose flour, baking powder, and salt in a small bowl; set aside. Stir together the boiling water and ¼ teaspoon of the espresso powder in a cup until the espresso is completely dissolved. Whisk together the cocoa, hot espresso mixture, and vanilla in a medium bowl; set aside.

3 Put the chocolate in a small microwavable bowl and microwave on High until melted, about 40 seconds. Whisk in the oil until smooth. Whisk in the sucralose–brown sugar blend until combined. Whisk the chocolate mixture into the cocoa mixture; whisk in the beaten egg until combined. Add the flour mixture and walnuts (if using) and stir just until blended.

4 Pour the batter into the pan. Bake until a toothpick inserted into the center comes out with a few moist crumbs clinging, 9–10 minutes. Let cool completely in the pan on a rack.

5 To make the glaze, stir together the remaining ½ teaspoon of espresso powder and the hot milk in a cup until the espresso is completely dissolved. Add the confectioners' sugar and stir until the mixture forms a smooth paste. Using a spoon, drizzle the glaze over the brownies. Cut into 12 bars.

PER SERVING (1 brownie): 79 Cal, 4 g Fat, 1 g Sat Fat, 0 g Trans Fat, 18 mg Chol, 51 mg Sod, 11 g Carb, 1 g Fib, 2 g Prot, 20 mg Calc. *POINTS* value: *2.*

How We Did It We like to make these brownies by hand using a whisk and spatula. If you prefer to use an electric mixer, beat together all the ingredients except the flour mixture and walnuts. Then stir in the flour mixture and walnuts using a wooden spoon just until combined.

Creamy Almond-Apricot Brown Rice Pudding

HANDS-ON PREP 10 MIN   COOK 15 MIN   SERVES 4

2   cups cooked instant brown rice
1½ cups protein-fortified fat-free milk
3   tablespoon finely chopped dried apricots
½   cup fat-free half-and-half
1   teaspoon packed sucralose–brown sugar
    blend or 2 teaspoons packed brown sugar
¼   teaspoon almond extract
Pinch nutmeg (optional)

1 Combine rice, milk, and apricots in a medium saucepan and set over medium-high heat; bring just to a boil. Reduce the heat to medium-low. Cook, covered, stirring, until most of the milk is absorbed, 12–15 minutes.

2 Remove the saucepan from the heat. Stir in the half-and-half, sucralose–brown sugar blend, and almond extract; set aside until the rice pudding is creamy looking, 2–3 minutes. Divide the pudding evenly among 4 custard cups and sprinkle with the nutmeg (if using). Serve warm or refrigerate, covered, to serve chilled later.

PER SERVING (½ cup pudding): 177 Cal, 1 g Fat, 1 g Sat Fat, 0 g Trans Fat, 3 mg Chol, 358 mg Sod, 35 g Carb, 4 g Fib, 7 g Prot, 158 mg Calc. **POINTS** value: **3.**

How We Did It   This rice pudding is best when wonderfully creamy. If it stands too long and gets drier than desired, simply stir in a bit of water until moistened to your taste. The pudding can also be topped with fat-free sour cream that has been sweetened with a touch of sucralose.

Chocolate-Coconut Pudding

HANDS-ON PREP 5 MIN   COOK 15 MIN   SERVES 4

- ¼ cup unsweetened cocoa powder
- 2 tablespoons sucralose-sugar blend or ¼ cup granulated sugar
- 2 tablespoons cornstarch
- 2¼ cups fat-free milk
- ½ teaspoon coconut extract
- 4 teaspoons unsweetened flaked coconut, toasted

1 Preheat the oven to 350°F.

2 Whisk together the cocoa, sucralose-sugar blend, and cornstarch in a heavy medium saucepan; slowly whisk in the milk and set over medium-high heat. Cook, stirring constantly, until the pudding comes to a boil. Reduce the heat to medium and cook until thickened, about 5 minutes. Remove the saucepan from the heat and stir in the coconut extract. Divide the pudding evenly among 4 dessert dishes; let cool 5 minutes.

3 Sprinkle 1 teaspoon of the coconut over each pudding. Serve immediately or refrigerate, covered, up to 1 day.

PER SERVING (½ cup pudding): 110 Cal, 2 g Fat, 2 g Sat Fat, 0 g Trans Fat, 3 mg Chol, 60 mg Sod, 20 g Carb, 2 g Fib, 6 g Prot, 180 mg Calc. **POINTS** value: **2.**

How We Did It   To toast the coconut: Line a toaster-oven tray with foil. Sprinkle the coconut evenly on the tray and toast until golden brown, about 3 minutes. Or spread the coconut in a small skillet and cook over medium heat, stirring, until golden.

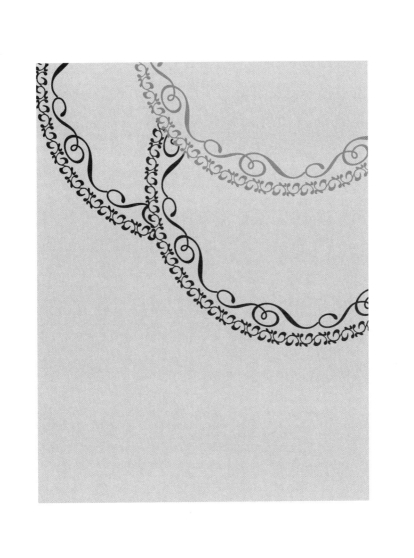

RICOTTA CHEESE TART
WITH CANDIED ORANGE PEEL,
PAGE 50

Dry and Liquid Measurement Equivalents

If you are converting the recipes in this book to metric measurements, use the following chart as a guide.

TEASPOONS	TABLESPOONS	CUPS	FLUID OUNCES
3 teaspoons	1 tablespoon		½ fluid ounce
6 teaspoons	2 tablespoons	⅛ cup	1 fluid ounce
8 teaspoons	2 tablespoons plus 2 teaspoons	⅙ cup	
12 teaspoons	4 tablespoons	¼ cup	2 fluid ounces
15 teaspoons	5 tablespoons	⅓ cup minus 1 teaspoon	
16 teaspoons	5 tablespoons plus 1 teaspoon	⅓ cup	
18 teaspoons	6 tablespoons	¼ cup plus 2 tablespoons	3 fluid ounces
24 teaspoons	8 tablespoons	½ cup	4 fluid ounces
30 teaspoons	10 tablespoons	½ cup plus 2 tablespoons	5 fluid ounces
32 teaspoons	10 tablespoons plus 2 teaspoons	⅔ cup	
36 teaspoons	12 tablespoons	¾ cup	6 fluid ounces
42 teaspoons	14 tablespoons	1 cup minus 2 tablespoons	7 fluid ounces
45 teaspoons	15 tablespoons	1 cup minus 1 tablespoon	
48 teaspoons	16 tablespoons	1 cup	8 fluid ounces

VOLUME	
¼ teaspoon	1 milliliter
½ teaspoon	2 milliliters
1 teaspoon	5 milliliters
1 tablespoon	15 milliliters
2 tablespoons	30 milliliters
3 tablespoons	45 milliliters
¼ cup	60 milliliters
⅓ cup	80 milliliters
½ cup	120 milliliters
⅔ cup	160 milliliters
¾ cup	175 milliliters
1 cup	240 milliliters
1 quart	950 milliliters

LENGTH	
1 inch	25 millimeters
1 inch	2.5 centimeters

OVEN TEMPERATURE			
250°F	120°C	400°F	200°C
275°F	140°C	425°F	220°C
300°F	150°C	450°F	230°C
325°F	160°C	475°F	250°C
350°F	180°C	500°F	260°C
375°F	190°C	525°F	270°C

WEIGHT	
1 ounce	30 grams
¼ pound	120 grams
½ pound	240 grams
1 pound	480 grams

NOTE: Measurement of less than ⅛ teaspoon is considered a dash or a pinch. Metric volume measurements are approximate.

Recipe Index

C

POINTS value Recipe Index